D1580891

THE POSITIVE PUPPY

TRAINING BLUEPRINT

An 8 Week Step-By-Step Action Plan To Raise The Perfect Dog Using Proven Loving & Friendly Methods

SAM QUINN

TABLE OF CONTENTS

YOUR FREE GIFT

As a way of saying **thank you** for your purchase, I am offering you an additional, very useful information document on 2 specific puppy topics. Hope you like it!

- A Puppy Development Schedule (from birth to 4 years old)

- A Socialization List (things you might not think of when socializing your pup)

Scan the QR-code to easily get your FREE gift
https://pebblepublishingllc.activehosted.com/f/3

FACEBOOK GROUP

Welcome to the Tribe!

If you want to get even more informative insights you can always
join my Facebook group:

New Puppy & Dog Owners Tribe

(https://www.facebook.com/groups/dogownerstribe)

Scan the QR-code to easily join the Facebook Group

Prologue

James and Pepper's Story

Whether or not you've trained before, you've probably seen them: those big, irresistible puppy eyes. They're adorable, pleading, and very hard to ignore. Above all else, they usually show up after they've made a mess, right around the time you find it. What a coincidence.

A pup that's too cute to be angry at may be frustrating, but often enough, that's the least of your problems during the early weeks of training. Biting, chewing, and barking are just a few symptoms of a puppy gone wild, but what does that mean? Are some puppies impossible to train or naturally prone to bad behavior? Should you just give up? Of course not! Dogs are a lot of work at every age, but most difficult behaviors are a result of incorrect or insufficient training. By training your puppy right from the start and working with their natural developmental stages, you can get ahead of these problems on their schedule.

James brought a brand new puppy named Pepper into his home at just eight weeks old. He thought he was ready to own a dog but didn't have any experience with training such a young pup. At eight weeks, he had a lot of expectations for what Pepper would be able to handle. He decided to get everything out of the way early on, showing her where to go to the bathroom, letting her roam free in the backyard, and giving her new commands every day. Right away, he ran into some problems.

Most of the time, Pepper just didn't seem to understand what she was supposed to do. She would go potty in the right spot one day and then ruin her kennel the next. In the yard, she would go absolutely crazy, and it was impossible to convince her to come back inside when it was time to settle down. When she was told to sit, she'd sit and then get right back up and bark for treats. She even found the treat bag one night and ripped it open, making a huge mess and getting herself sick.

James thought that things would get better along the way. By one month in, though, nothing had improved. She would chew on everything in the house no matter how many times he said 'no!' and he couldn't get her to stay still on her leash during walks. When she got upset, he didn't know what to do to calm her down, other than give her some treats. Soon enough, Pepper learned that barking and throwing a fit would get her as many treats as she wanted. This wasn't good for James or Pepper in the long run.

Months later, James was exhausted by his puppy. He could never control her, she didn't like to spend time with him, and every night was another mess to clean up. He finally decided that he had adopted an untrainable dog and brought her back to the shelter to return her.

The worst part about this situation is that Pepper never understood what the problem was. James might have had good intentions along the way, but he didn't communicate with Pepper in a way that made any sense in the mind of a puppy.

At first, she was allowed outside for as long as she wanted. She learned that it was okay to run around in the yard all day if she wanted, so when James called for her to come back in, she didn't know what that meant. Then, when the leash came into the picture, she couldn't move very easily, and that was scary. James would tell her to do things like sit, stay, shake, and fetch, but as soon as she got good at one of them, he'd move on to the next thing, and she hardly got any practice. One day she gets treats for sitting still; the next, she gets them for running around. What was she supposed to think?

When her teeth started to grow in, she felt like she had to chew, and then she didn't understand what to do when James started yelling. If she was bad for chewing the chair, maybe the carpet was okay? Everything here was just so complicated. Whenever she tried to show that she was confused or scared, she'd get more treats. This taught her that it was a good thing to bark loudly when things felt weird, and they felt weird a lot.

The day that James put her in the car and took her back to the shelter, she barked and barked a lot, but there were no treats this time. Instead, she was left alone with a bunch of other dogs and strangers and never saw James again. As she got older, she tried to use what she learned with her new owners, and they didn't understand it at all. They thought her barking and chewing was bad, but that's not what she learned when she was a puppy! How was she ever supposed to get things right, now?

The mind of a puppy works very differently from a human child's mind, but what they have in common is that they learn and grow over time. At a very young age, puppies may learn something about their environment that makes them develop a behavior that is hard to get rid of in later years. This often comes through a form of action/reaction processing, which is core to the way dogs think and understand the world.

When something new or unusual happens near a puppy, they will act in a way that feels natural. How you react as their master will reinforce whether or not their action was good or bad. If they think they did something correctly, they will repeat it the next time the stimulus happens. If they think they did something incorrectly, they will try something new in the future. In a good training environment, this cycle continues, and they learn a little quicker every time. Eventually, a puppy can be smart enough to guess the correct behavior on a new task before being redirected.

Unfortunately, I can't promise this will get rid of those troublesome puppy-dog eyes. Your pup is bound to make messes and mistakes here and there, and they'll give you that look when you find them. With a well-trained dog, this is actually a sign that they know they did something wrong and empathize with your reaction. It means they will learn from this mistake and do better next time, and you should take it as a sign that your puppy is trying its best.

Introduction

Fur-st things First

Anew puppy can take many forms: a new friend, a new experience, and a whole lot of new work. To train your pup right, you need to keep all of these things in mind along the way. This is a life-long relationship in the making, and it doesn't come without effort on your end too. By starting dogs off on the right paw, they'll learn to look to you for guidance and trust your judgment when you have to correct their behavior. This strong bond is largely built during the first eight weeks of your puppy training.

That is why having all of the tips, tricks, and expectations laid out on a week-by-week basis is a necessary tool to maximize the effectiveness of your training. This book is designed on that exact principle. I have laid out a week-by-week action plan for the first eight weeks of dog training, starting with an eight-week-old puppy. Each week will highlight major goals for training, created with the puppy's developmental stages in mind. Like this, you can schedule your training in a way that won't over-stimulate your puppy and effectively paces itself in a comfortable way for both of you.

Every week of puppy training will teach you new things about your little pal's process and personality. The guide will slowly introduce new techniques and instructions for a variety of essential training exercises while recapping everything you've learned in prior chapters. Each week will build upon the last, giving you room to grow and use repetition to practice previous lessons. You will always want to repeat new activities with your puppies on a regular schedule so that your pup knows what is expected of them when they enter training mode and can take their newly learned skills into their daily life with or without your help.

This guide is designed to start with a puppy that is already eight weeks old. Experts believe that this is the ideal time to bring home a new dog and begin forming a bond between master and pet. Your puppy will be able to walk, bark, and understand basic training exercises at this stage. They'll also be excited about understanding and experiencing the world, so you should definitely be a part of their exploration. From 8-16 weeks, these step-by-step exercises will establish the necessary building blocks for your pup to grow into an obedient and intelligent adult dog.

If you happen to have a dog that's older than eight weeks, whether it's a little or a lot, this guide will still work for you. The eight-week guideline for adoption is the ideal situation, but we all know it isn't the only possibility of getting the perfect pup. Sometimes, a pup needs a little extra time before they can be adopted or had a rough start in another home. No matter how old your puppy is, this guide will still get you through the basics and start your training off right.

Each Session Counts

This book is set up as a week-by-week action plan rather than a standalone collection of tips. Following the guide correctly means you should use it week-by-week, without skipping weeks or cherry-picking parts that seem interesting to you. For most puppies, this will set the right pacing to follow the lessons and retain the information without being over-stimulated or rushed into difficult new tasks.

Now, some pups are fast learners. Suppose your particular puppy seems to be getting bored with doing the same lesson over and over again, or you're confident that they have the exercise figured out. In that case, nothing is stopping you from skipping ahead to the next week a little early. Just make sure that your dog is ready for the new material and is excited to try the new stuff.

The Positive Puppy Training Blueprint is set up on this schedule because the first two months (eight weeks) of a puppy's training career is **the most important time** for learning. This window is **the best time** to imprint everything you want in a pup's mind without having to retrain on the basics. This guide works with that knowledge to create a framework that's easy for puppies to follow and people to see the results they want to see.

The Adventure Begins

When you're ready to start this journey with you and your new best friend, you will want to have everything prepared to start training right away. This means checking that your gear, environment, and attitude are all in order.

To get ready, make sure you have all the gear you need. This checklist can be used to make sure you've covered the basics that will be used in this guide and other basic puppy-care needs:

- ✓ Food and water bowls
- ✓ Kennel
- ✓ Soft bed
- ✓ Treats
- ✓ Chew toys
- ✓ Ball or another fetch toy
- ✓ Other toys
- ✓ Puppy collar
- ✓ Long and short leash
- ✓ Puppy playpen

Next up, you'll want to prepare your training environment. Letting them have free reign of everything while you're trying to train isn't good for the pup or your sense of control. To start off, each training session should occur in the same place, and it should be somewhere inside your house. This means there will be no distractions, no hiding places, and no strangers. Your puppy's attention will be all yours, and they will be focused on what you are telling them to do. This environment should also be somewhere with enough space to move around, in a place you don't mind the puppy being. If there are any unexpected messes, you'll want the training environment to be a space where that is okay with you.

Gradually, you can expand your training environment to include other locations. As you introduce new tasks, you may need more space so that you can set up an "outside training zone" in your yard or at the park. When house training for certain tasks, you might want to train them on how to interact in a particular room, with groups of people, or in specific locations like the car. The training environment should only be expanded like this when your dog has demonstrated an ability to stay focused during training and that they can handle potential distractions involved in moving to a new place.

Finally, the part that is most important… to your puppy, at least: the treats! Getting a good type of treat before you begin training is vital for setting high expectations in your puppy's eyes. If you've got something they want, you want them to know that on day one of training. This will make them excited to perform well and get those rewards.

Your training treats should ideally be different than any other treats you give them for less important rewards. They should be highly desirable and small enough that you can give them a few in a row without making them sick. These are called "high reward" treats, for reasons you can probably guess. Good examples you can keep around the house are small cut-up pieces of hot dog or chicken, but you can find specialized dog treats designed for training at most pet stores.

Rules to Live By

The most vital things you will learn while training your puppy extend outside the limits of the exercises themselves. Before training begins, you need to understand a few key elements that will make the experience better for everyone involved: **fun, positive reinforcement, corrections, patience, consistency, and repetition.** These are core principles to healthy, positive dog training that each chapter will refer back to during the step-by-step exercises and guidance.

First and most importantly, every training session should be fun for your puppy. It should be **fun** for you too, but especially for the pup. They should learn that training is a good time and be excited for it to begin every day. This will keep them interested in you and attentive to the tasks at hand while making their minds associate the exercises themselves with positive feelings. If training is boring, upsetting, or confusing, they won't want to do their best, and they'll be more focused on getting to the end of it than learning anything meaningful.

This affects the second rule in a similar way. The action plan you will follow over the next eight weeks works under the framework of **positive reinforcement** training with healthy corrections integrated to set boundaries. Positive reinforcement training works on the basis of understanding that your dog will always learn better from getting a reward than getting a harsh punishment. A puppy's mind understands that good behavior will reap good benefits, and they will try to do that good behavior as long as they understand what it is. If your puppy continues to make the same mistakes during training, it isn't because they don't want to complete the task correctly. It is because they do not understand when they are doing the right thing. This guide will give you the right tools to use positive reinforcement as the core of your training sessions, making for the most efficient and healthy learning environment possible.

From time to time, **corrections** may still be needed to see that you and your dog are on the same page. The word 'corrections' may sound scary for those who do not want to hurt or upset the dog. Within this guide's methodology, minor corrections are used to indicate where boundaries for your dog lie for the sake of their safety and understanding. You will never be instructed to hit, hurt, or abuse your dog in any way. The use of corrections should always be on terms your dog will understand to redirect them away from bad or dangerous behavior and reinforce that it is not acceptable. In each training exercise throughout this guide, you will be given examples of when it is appropriate to use gentle corrections for the sake of training, and how to make sure it still creates a positive environment for you to build a trusting relationship between you and your puppy.

If this word still makes you nervous, worry not. Later sections of this guide will explain the difference between "positive reinforcement" and "negative reinforcement" within the realm of dog training. There is also a separation between "positive punishment" and "negative punishment." The word punishment is not necessarily intended to bring thoughts of fearful dogs and harsh treatment. In positive dog training, punishment and corrections are never used to dominate the dog. Instead, they are used to redirect their attention and make an association between right and wrong. Healthy punishments can include removing a problematic toy, temporarily restricting access to a reward, or moving the dog away from an incorrect focus. These are always done in the moment of the behavior and should never be prolonged for long periods. Productive corrections happen at the moment of the 'wrong' action so that your puppy can know what the problem was. Punishing your puppy for long periods is not a correction that they will understand.

Next, you need to remember that these weeks are laid out week-by-week, but every puppy catches onto things at a different rate. Your pup might be a quick learner, and you can look ahead to introduce new tasks a little bit earlier. In some cases, your dog might also need some time and **patience** to learn a specific task. Your job is not to push your puppy through these exercises as fast as possible. Rushing will never make for better training or understanding in the long run; in fact, it only hurts the process. Getting them to learn a task and moving on too quickly can make it hard for them to retain the information, and lose all the progress you made after a long session. If something doesn't work today, you can always try again tomorrow. Repetition is more valuable than rushing when it comes to the "eager to please" mind of a puppy.

This is why **consistency** is essential. If you decide to use the word 'come' as your command for the puppy to run towards you, you can't start to use 'here' as the command halfway through and expect the same results. Bringing the same language, environment, toys, and tools to each training session will help your dog connect the dots between what you want them to do and how they should behave.

Finally, you must be prepared to use **repetition** as one of the most vital tools at your disposal throughout puppy training. Each exercise in this guide will show you the steps you need to make a valuable training session work for you and your puppy, but they are not magic. Training something just once will not work for most dogs. Did you pick up algebra after the first problem you ever solved?

The more you work on one small command, response, or behavior, the more natural it will be for your dog to do it on their own with little to no extra guidance from you. Incorporating these elements and following these rules will make it possible for you to get the most value out of each session.

Barking Up the First Tree (weeks 8-9)

This first week is crucial to the development of your puppy and the relationship they have with training. The 8-16 week period of growth is the best period for pups to be introduced to their people and environment, as they are most impressionable at this age. Getting it right from week one will make the rollercoaster ride of ups and downs throughout weeks 2-16 a lot smoother. This is the most intense period of their young doggy lives, and you're there to get them through it, one way or another.

Understanding this when you begin training will make the entire process easier. Each week of a puppy's early life is going to be different from the last. Just like with people, young dogs go through more change and development in the first few months than they will for the rest of their life. Getting to know your puppy one phase at a time will make it seem like you have a completely different dog today than you did a week ago, but that's okay. This period is just as exciting for them as it will be for you if you open your mind up to the positivity of the experience.

'What do dogs do on their day off? Can't lie around— that's their job.'

- GEORGE CARLIN

For this reason, I provided a developmental diagram as an extra freebie to this book package. Go to the 'Your free gift' page at the beginning of the book to find more details on how to download it.

The focus of your training this week should center around all of the most crucial starter steps to beginning a productive, long-term relationship with your puppy. Bringing them home, introducing them to other dogs, using a crate, and all of the other necessities for day-to-day puppy life need to be introduced early on in order for them to understand it.

For all of these issues, you can use this guide as an active companion during training. That means that you can have the book in one hand, puppy in the other. Every goal is followed by a list of frequently asked questions, and a step-by-step guide to exactly what you need to do to tackle those problems hands-on.

Weekly Goal

This brings us to week one. For each session this week, you should show up with your end-goal in mind. It will set the tone for training and give you a place to ground things if you feel overwhelmed. As long as you focus and meet your goal, you can consider this first week a success, even if certain exercises or concepts need a little more practice to become perfect.

Week One Goal: Get the puppy comfortable in their new environment.

Comfort is the driving force behind making your puppy ready to learn and eager to please. This week, you want to get them comfortable with the new home, people, fellow dogs, and boundaries. You will want to tackle questions cropping up in your puppy's mind as they explore their new environment for the first time. Where to pee, when to eat, where to sleep, and everything else about their daily routine can be established within these first few days. The end goal should always be to keep your pup's comfort in mind as you sit down and show them their new world.

Where to Start

Even from the start, there is a lot your puppy needs to learn before they are thoroughly trained. Each training session will be packed full of exercises, repetition, and new information for you and your pup, but don't let that be the end of it. Above all else, your puppy should have fun while training. If they don't enjoy the process, you will never keep their full attention, and they will just waste your time until they are allowed to do something more interesting. Your training should always be the more exciting thing for them to do. If you start a session and your dog is eagerly waiting for you in the training environment, you're doing something right.

This is easier than it might sound. High-activity exercises are automatically engaging for most dogs because they are an excellent outlet for their natural wells of energy. Toys, treats, and your attention are three rewards that automatically come with most training exercises.

One way to keep things fun, even in the most exhausting exercises, is to implement a play session at the end of every training exercise. It's is a great reward that will teach your puppy that being good during work-time means extra-fun playtime afterward. It will keep their excitement up throughout the entire exercise, making them eager to come again the next day. It also ensures that your puppy is more likely to respond positively to you in general, because they know you're a lot of fun. This is great for deepening your bond early on.

Frequently Asked Questions and Training Steps

Let's get into frequent questions about the most vital early training exercises. Whether you've encountered these topics already or not, they are bound to come up along the way. Setting your expectations and having the necessary steps on hand will make training more comfortable as you figure out your puppy's needs.

What Should the House Rules Be?

Believe it or not, puppies understand rules. In fact, a dog's mind is built around them. Knowing what is right and what is wrong is the best way for you both to be on the same page. This is why it's important to make those rules in week one when your puppy is first learning the ropes. Your rules are up to you, but these basics are a necessity.

- Setting a routine is the most important way to solidify any rules that are important to you. In the first few weeks, keeping a consistent schedule will make it clear to your puppy what they should expect. If one person gets up in the morning and feeds them, that should happen at the same time, by the same person every day, if possible. Going outside, in the crate, and playtime should all happen at regular times throughout the day.

- If the dog wants to roam outside of their designated puppy zone, bring them back to their area. This can be a big issue when it comes to potty training and other early exercises you want your puppy to focus on. You might need to use a puppy pen or gates to keep the pup from wandering around the whole house.

Ultimately, you need to come up with your own rules based on what is important to you. Some people are fine with having the puppy on certain furniture pieces, and some people are not. I will give you an example of the doggy rules I set first in my house. Then, you can use the blank lines to write down your own and put them somewhere to remind everyone what the deal is.

Sam Quinn's Rules

- Choose a quiet place to put the crate

- Choose a place where the puppy will eat

- The couch and bed are off-limits (don't give in to those cute puppy eyes, stay strong!)

- Assign a designated pee and poop area in the garden

- Choose the areas in the house the puppy can roam, and which are off-limits

Now it's your turn, take a moment to think about the house rules you want your puppy to abide by from the start. You can write them down here.

_____

_____

_____

_____

_____

_____

_____

_____

_____

_____

_____

_____

What Is the First Thing I Should Do When I Bring My Pup Home?

It is normal to be excited when your puppy first arrives at home. They'll be excited too. They will be very, *very* excited. This might seem like a chaotic time, where you will be tempted to let your pup do whatever they want for the sake of simplicity. As appealing as this may seem, resist the urge to let that puppy go wild. This moment is essential for imprinting the right boundaries on your puppy, and there are a few things you can do to ensure that it is as successful as possible.

These are the most important tips to help you start off right as soon as paws hit the floor. Use this as a checklist as soon as you get home and the dog days have begun.

1. Bring them outside to pee in the designated area of the yard.

This is the best way to begin your puppy's potty-training journey with the rules laid out clearly. When dogs get used to a new area, their instincts want them to mark it as new territory. Yes, this usually means peeing. If you bring them to the yard right away and show them the "potty spot," they will instinctually mark it as their own. This forms the right association with relieving themselves outside, rather than where it is unwelcome (Reisen, 2020).

When they inevitably do, take this time for your very first training moment. As soon as they start to 'go,' use the command you'll eventually want them to associate with this. It can be 'go potty' or 'go outside' or something like 'bye-bye,' as long as you plan to keep it consistent for each command. Doing this every time your puppy goes in the right place will help them associate the two. By forming this pattern from the beginning, when you want them to take a bathroom break, you can use that key phrase, and they will know where they're supposed to be.

2. Limit where they can roam.

At first, you will want to reign in your puppy's expectations about where they are allowed to go. You might be eager to have them following you all over the house, but it is important to set limits in the beginning stages (Reisen, 2020). If you let your puppy roam around the house freely, they may become over-stimulated and confused. They will be introduced to so many new smells, places, sights, and people, that they will have a hard time mapping out their new home. This will make them very uncomfortable and more likely to be afraid than relaxed. In some cases, it might even trigger their territorial instincts, and they will want to make as many new potty places as they can find. This is not what you want on your first day with the new puppy.

When you bring them inside for the first time, show them the areas they are allowed to enter. Keep this limited to one part of the house at first, where you can keep an eye on them, and they can get used to the activity going on around him. You can still allow them to explore and make themselves at home, but this should be within a designated boundary. It can be the same room as the crate, food, and water so that they have everything they need right away (Reisen, 2020). You should have an area in mind ahead of time and put some thought into it before dog day begins. That way, it can be all set and done, and everything is prepared for when the puppy comes home.

Over time, you can introduce the rest of the house piece by piece. Doing this in phases will let them get used to each one on their own terms. This will keep your dog from being as rowdy, destructive, or scared as it might be if the locations are too overwhelming. If an area is off-limits to your pup, don't show it to them. They will learn over time that there is a reason that room is unfamiliar to them.

3. Introduce the family.

If you live with any other humans, you will want to make sure they meet the puppy on day one. This will establish them as part of the pack and part of their new home, instead of potential strangers. You should always take leadership and be there with your puppy as they meet the others. No matter how many people live in the house, you should take this step slowly and keep your puppy's comfort in mind at all times. Every part of your puppy's first day at home should be pleasant and fun.

You will want to handle these introductions one at a time if possible. There is a good chance that your family is just as excited to see the new puppy as you are, so if more than one person wants to meet them at a time, try to limit how many people are right in front of the puppy's face. You should give the pup a chance to individually meet each family member in a quiet, relaxed environment (Reisen, 2020). Excitement can produce loud voices, erratic movements, and too much touching. While this might be okay later on in your puppy's life, it will be scary on this first day full of new things.

Each meeting should be in your designated dog zone and on the pup's terms. Kneeling down to their level and letting them come to you is a great way to make sure they feel like they are in control. Having a toy with you can also make the meeting fun and form a positive association with the family from the beginning.

4. Show them their quiet place.

The first few days in a new home are exhausting for anyone, pup or person. No matter how much your puppy likes you, they're going to get tired, and they might get a little overwhelmed from their big day. This is a great time to introduce the crate, which is their place to retreat to for a little bit of privacy and rest. By showing it to them right away, they will know it is a safe option for them later on. This will make the entire crate training experience more comforting for the puppy and easier for you in the long-run.

Puppies sleep anywhere from 15 hours to 20 hours a day (Reisen, 2020). They are constantly expending energy, and they need a lot of time to recuperate. If the pup is familiar with their crate from day one, they will know it is a safe place to sleep later and get those essential hours of rest. After a day of introductions and exploration, take your puppy to the crate when they start to get tuckered out. They'll probably want to take a nap, and the security of their den will make them associate it with safety.

We'll go over the specific steps to crate training in the next section, but don't be afraid to introduce it as one of the first things after coming home. The crate is not a punishment; it is their personal den to retreat to when the rest of the house is chaotic. They should be familiar with it right away, as this will make them feel safe when it is time for them to stay in the crate throughout the training period.

5. Be prepared for problems.

No puppy arrival is perfect, but that doesn't mean there's something wrong with the puppy. No matter how much you prepare, there is bound to be something that goes wrong. That's okay. Everything is fixable, and this is just another part of the adventure of getting a new best friend. There are a few common hiccups that many people experience when introducing a pup to the home for the first time. If you know what to expect, there are proven ways to troubleshoot these problems and get ahead of the chaos.

Unexplained Accidents

First of all, your puppy is going to be excited… a lot. That is ultimately a good thing, because that high-energy attitude is a dog's way of expressing happiness, and they will likely be happy to see you from the beginning. Sometimes, when a puppy is excited, they forget some of their newly learned bathroom training. Yes, this means that they might get so thrilled when you come home that they start to pee… all over the house. This is a relatively common occurrence with young dogs still potty training, and it doesn't mean that they are failing to learn. It merely means that they aren't in complete control of their reactions yet, and might need a little extra attention.

If this becomes a regular occurrence, you can combat this by changing up your routine. First, identify the trigger point. For example, this might be when you come home from work and come to let them out of the crate. Instead of doing things as normal during this moment, start implementing a "potty break" time at this same moment. When you come home, bring them outside to pee immediately, using your practiced command phrase. It might not work right away, but with repetition, your puppy will learn to expect a potty break when you get home from work. This will train them to wait until they are outside to pee rather than let their body take over right away. Over time, this routine will make them feel calmer when you get home, and make it less of an intense moment for everyone involved.

Do I Really Need a Crate for My Puppy?

Many new dog owners are wary of using a crate for their dogs. This largely comes from the misconception that a crate is synonymous with "puppy jail," and is only used to restrict your pet. Contrary to popular belief, this is absolutely not the case.

There is no need to feel guilty for crate training your pup. Canines of all types, domestic and wild, crave an enclosed shelter. This is commonly referred to as a 'den.' Dogs are descendants of wild wolves, and their instincts make them seek a den-like space to feel protected from unknown elements. This is the purpose a crate serves in domestic training. Professionals like trainers, breeders, and vets insist that crate training dogs from a young age prevents more behavioral problems than not (Arford, 2019).

A good crate should not be considered a cage. Instead, it should be regarded as an area of protection for your puppy to make their own. When you prepare the puppy crate, you should have their comfort in mind. Ideally, the crate should have three solid sides, and one open side on the front, making it feel more like a cave than a box. If you can't get a crate built like this, you can cover the extra sides with a blanket or a towel. This gives the dog a feeling of enclosure and safety, knowing that they are hidden from any potential threats while in their den.

You should also make sure there is a soft bed in the crate. A crate with a hard floor is uncomfortable. This can be a pet bed or a pile of blankets, as long as you sincerely think it will be comfortable for your pup. They will be sleeping and relaxing in here when you're gone. How would you feel if you arrived at your new home and found that your bedroom didn't have a bed inside?

Another small trick you can use to help your pup feel safe and comfortable is to put something from the original nest in the crate. This might be a rag or a blanket, an item that bears the scent of its mother and littermates. If you don't have access to that, you can also substitute this with a T-shirt carrying your scent.

Crate training is also a great way to reinforce other early training topics in your dog's mind. When puppies feel safe in their crate, they won't soil it by peeing inside. This means that they will hold their bladder during the time spent in the crate. By solidifying a routine where the pup is in the crate overnight or while you are at work, you are also teaching them a pattern. This will help them establish when it is time to go potty and other important parts of their daily schedule.

If you find that your puppy is still peeing in the crate, there may be other issues at play. When a crate is too large for a puppy, they might consider some parts of the crate 'okay' to pee in, because they aren't the parts they sleep in. Make sure that the crate is the right size for your puppy if there are frequent accidents. And remember that they can only hold their bladder one hour per month of age.

Without a crate, a lot of problems can surface between your puppy's understanding of their environment and your expectations of their behavior. If the pup has nowhere safe to rest when you are out of the house or asleep, they will have full reign over the house to chew, run, pee, and destroy. There is only so much you can train them to do early on, and they will cause more damage when unattended if they don't have a place of their own. More importantly, the crate serves a vital role in handling emergencies or uncertain situations. If you need to get your puppy out of the house at a moment's notice, having them crate-trained makes it easy to get them under control and removed from the situation without hassle (Arford, 2019). In the case of a fire, medical emergency, or another stressful scenario, a loose dog will only add to the danger. On a more positive note though, if you've booked a weekend away with your loved one and want to bring the dog with you, a crate is the best way to go. Because you don't want to get that hotel bill on Monday morning, saying you have to pay for everything your dog broke during your stay, right?!

Aside from that, ever heard of 'separation anxiety'? It's a very much talked about topic that scares a lot of new dog owners. Nobody wants to end up with a dog that cannot be left alone at home. Crate training is a vital part in preventing this behavior, this is why it's important to begin crate training in week one. Follow these steps, and use the crate to build trust between the dog and their environment.

To recap, your puppy should only be out of it's crate to poop and pee or for a training or play session with you. In between all of these moments, your puppy should be crated. This will prevent your pup from creating bad habits like chewing on furniture, peeing all over the house or following you around everywhere. Having said that, you probably read between the lines that you need to work your puppy multiple times a day, because otherwise they are just living a crated life and that's not at all what we want. Once they get a little bit older, you can phase out the crate bit by bit.

Depending on the personality and character of your dog, crating might last up to 2 years before you can trust them without it. If you're one of the lucky ones you might be able to get rid of the crate after a year. But don't be discouraged if that's not the case. I still crate my dogs from time to time when I notice that they are slacking in obedience training. Even though my dogs are now 4 and 5 years old, well trained and not in need of a crate anymore, sometimes I need to go back to basics to get back on track with training. Dotting the I's and crossing some T's never hurt anyone, you know!

Steps to Crate Training

The crate should be somewhere in your house where the family spends time, not isolated or out of the way. They should always feel like they are part of the social group when they are in the crate, even if they are seeking privacy.

1. Before you start this exercise, your puppy must be comfortable on the leash. So skip ahead to the next FAQ '*How Should I Put On The Leash for Training?*', and then come back.

2. Introduce the crate. Bring the puppy to the crate and throw treats in the back of the crate. Let the dog run after them and keep the door open during this time. Do **not** shove them inside or force them to go in all the way.

3. The tossing of the treats will encourage them to go inside, even if they do not go in all the way at first. Continue this tossing game until there is no hesitation anymore to go inside the crate. This could work right away or take a few days. Eventually, your puppy should feel comfortable going inside on its own. Remember to not shut the door yet, but to let them come out again and get their reward.

4. Rinse and repeat multiple times.

5. Now it's time to mark the behavior with 'kennel' or 'place' or whatever word you want to use.

6. Keep a treat in your hand and point to the kennel, say 'kennel' but don't throw the treat yet. Some dogs will walk right in, others won't. If they don't, give them time to think for themselves. Puppy still doesn't want to go in, that's when you help again by tossing the treat in again. Try this until they get it. If they go in, throw them a big party because now you have a breakthrough!

7. Now they are ready for the next step, closing the door. Ask them to go in the kennel, throw in a couple of treats and close the door. Walk a few steps away from the kennel and come back when they are done eating the treats. This will slowly introduce them to the

idea that the door might close. If you go back to open the door, make sure the dog doesn't bolt out. If they try to do that, close the door again to make them back up and say 'wait'. If they wait, mark it with 'good' and afterwards release them with 'break'.

8. Over the next few attempts, lengthen the time that you keep the door closed. Put the puppy in, throw some treats and walk away. Go back to the crate, throw in some more treats and walk away again. Start slow and build up to a couple of minutes, then a few more, until they can stay in the crate for 10-15 minutes after getting their treat.

9. Respect the rules of crate training. There are a few things you should **never** do if you want your dog to have a healthy relationship with the crate. Never use it as a punishment. If they only get locked in the crate when they are bad, they will associate the area with fear instead of safety. Never leave them in the crate for too long. For puppies under the age of six months, you should not leave them in the crate for more than four hours at a time. Even as they get older, you should not leave a dog in the crate all day (The Humane Society, 2018).

10. Graduation. Over time, your puppy will get more and more comfortable in the crate, and you can teach them to stay in there with the door open.

How Should I Put on the Leash for Training?

A leash is a vital tool for you to introduce your puppy to the complex world around them without the risk of running off or getting into something they shouldn't. The problem is that not every puppy understands what a leash is, and getting it on them can be a little bit of a struggle. If you positively introduce the leash with these starter steps, they will be more likely to form a positive relationship with the tool.

1. Introduce the puppy to the collar and leash without putting it on them. Start off by letting them wear the collar by itself while they walk around the house. Let them eat in it, sleep in it, play in it, or anything else that they seem comfortable with.

2. Add the leash. You can first hook the leash to the collar and let them walk around without holding onto it. If they look at you or come towards you, give them a treat. They should be rewarded for paying attention to you while the leash is attached.

3. When the puppy comes towards you on their own, step back slightly and give them a treat for following you.

4. Practice walking around with the leash in hand, but do it inside. In their familiar territory, they should learn that the leash is safe and comfortable.

5. Finally, take it outside. Start off in the yard, with simple tasks such as going to the bathroom spot. Every time the puppy follows you, stays nearby, or otherwise behaves correctly, give them a treat.

Practice this every time you need to put the puppy on the leash. As they get used to wearing it, you can expand the places you go, the walks you take, and the looseness of the leash. We'll cover further leash training in week seven when your puppy is ready for more adventurous walks. For now, going on short walks around the block, preferably in an area where not many dogs visit. Your puppy isn't fully vaccinated yet, so you have to be careful.

What Are the Rules When It's Feeding Time?

Feeding can be overwhelming at first, for both puppy and person. Getting to eat is exciting! It can be tempting to let your puppy do whatever they want and focus on good manners later. In reality, food training should begin with the very first meal you serve.

It is important to set a few rules for behaving around food and implementing training into this exciting time of day. Food is an essential part of the puppy's routine and it comes with a natural reward. By establishing these rules upfront, your puppy will know when they behave correctly because they get to eat sooner.

- The puppy has to sit and wait until it's time to eat. They should not paw at the bowl, lick the bowl of other dogs, or jump at the food. Wait until they are sitting and behaving to give them the food, and they will start to do it automatically.

- If a treat or a piece of food drops on the floor, the puppy needs to learn to leave it alone. This is important to curb stealing food or eating toxic items that might look like a dropped treat. You can train your puppy to leave these items with the command words 'leave it.'

  - Place a piece of food or a treat in front of the pup while holding their collar or leash. Say 'leave it,' wait a few seconds, and then give the puppy a treat from your own hand. Repeat this, lengthening the amount of time between 'leave it' and the treat. Eventually, you can phase out the second treat because the puppy will know what 'leave it' means.

- Begging never gets a reward. If your puppy demonstrates whining, barking, or stealing around human food, don't give in.

How Can I Prevent My Dog From Peeing and Pooping Inside the House?

Small puppies need a lot of care during potty-training. At this age, they have a teeny tiny doggy bladder. This means that they need frequent trips outside to go to the bathroom. Even the most well-trained puppy might have accidents early on if you don't let them out often enough.

Here are some easy steps to make the most productive potty-training experience for you and your puppy.

1. Keep things on a schedule. We've said this before, but routines are everything in the puppy's mind. Outside of bathroom emergencies, you should set specific times that your pup knows they can go outside. Bringing them out after they wake up, after they eat, and other 'landmark' parts of the day is a great way to help their bladder get in tune.

2. In the beginning, bring them outside every 30-45 minutes. Over time, you can prolong this gap. Every week, this period can get a little longer, and you can establish the long-term schedule for potty-breaks.

3. Bring them outside on a leash, and lure them to the bathroom spot. Wait there until they go, at least five minutes, or longer if necessary.

4. If they go, give them a treat and mark the behavior with a phrase like 'good potty!' or whatever other phrase you would like to use. They should feel good for going on time, as this will help them form a regular habit.

5. If they don't go, bring them back inside, and put them in the crate for a little while. They are unlikely to have an accident in their crate, which will reinforce the fact that they missed their opportunity. Offer another chance after a short amount of time, and lead them to the pee spot again.

6. If it seems like they are always going outside to pee, this is a good thing. It might feel exhausting to go in and out all the time, but it is a good sign that they are going out to do their business. By teaching them that you will let them out when they 'ask,' or show signs of needing it, they will learn that they do not need to pee inside at all.

Most puppies take three to four months to develop a perfect bathroom schedule (Sydney, 2018). It might take a little while for them to get it right every time, so don't give up hope if it takes a little longer than that. There might be some hiccups along the way. This is normal. Potty training is one of the most difficult things a puppy will learn at this stage. You might have to get up in the middle of the night to let your puppy outside and prevent accidents. They need to go at least every five hours, so this is likely to be an issue at first. If they have a few mishaps, they may get confused about where they are supposed to go. If your pup keeps returning to the same place for an accident, restrict their access to it and deep clean. Until that scent is gone, their instincts will make them think it is the doggy bathroom.

My own pup, Nalu, took seven months to be potty trained. That's right, seven months! I wanted to give up many times throughout the experience, but I kept at our routine. I started to keep the door open at all times of the day when possible, letting her use the stairs to go outside by herself. This helped her learn that she always had the opportunity to go out to pee. The moral of this story is that every dog is a little different, and you might have to get creative to figure out the best way for your puppy to learn the rules.

How Should I Introduce the Puppy to My Other Pets?

If you have other pets already, you might be worried about whether or not they will get along with the new little brother or sister in the family. There are a few ways you can mitigate any conflict points by making sure their first meeting goes well. When the puppy comes home, go through these basic steps to make sure introductions are effective.

For Other Dogs

With dogs, there might be a little bit of friction when new pups enter the family. In many cases, it can go smoothly, with few problems along the way. In other cases, you can expect some growling, snapping, and other signs of hesitation when the dogs first meet. This is normal, and it doesn't mean they're going to hurt each other. In most cases, this results from a territory issue, or just because they have to get used to having another dog around.

- ◆ Ensure that all of your other dog's food, toys, water, etc., are out of the picture when the pup comes home. Just like people, dogs can get possessive of their things. If your dog sees the new kid messing with their favorite stuff, a rivalry might form. By getting all of their things out of the puppy zone, there is no particular property for the older dog to defend.

- ◆ Introduce them in a neutral environment at first. A dog park is a good example; the important part is that it is somewhere outside of your house. This will put them on equal territory when they first meet. They will have the chance to meet each other, get used to each other's scents, and become familiar. Then, when they encounter each other in the home, the older dog will feel less hostile about the new addition (Shojai, 2011). Then, bring them home with each on a leash. See how they interact on their own at first, and if there are problems, you can separate them with a fence, a closed door, or something else that lets them interact without being able to tussle too close.

- ◆ For the next steps, you can increase the amount of exposure between the two dogs over time. Try taking them on walks at the same time, or more visits to the park where they can play together. Eventually, when you want to have them in the same room of the house, let the dogs meet naturally (Shojai, 2011). Allow your dog to find the puppy in the house on their own, instead of forcing the meeting in an unnatural situation. You should still be there to monitor the meeting, but letting them interact on their own terms will set the right boundaries for their relationship.

Other Animals

When it comes to cats, rabbits, birds, and any other pets you might have in the house, the rules are slightly different. Dogs understand each other's behavior because they have the same instincts. A cat or a bird will confuse them at first because they will be viewing them through the lens of dog-be-havior. Your puppy will need some attentive care when being introduced to these strange, funny "other dogs" in their life.

◆ Start with your puppy in a confined area. You should already have a designated area to limit your puppy's exploration. Don't let your other pets in this area at first, so your puppy has it to themselves. If your other pets' food, water, or etc., are in this area, move them to another part of the house a week or two before the puppy's arrival. This will make it clear that there is no reason to go into the puppy zone in the near future.

◆ If your other pet lives in a cage or a terrarium, let your puppy come into the area when they are most relaxed. After a meal or playtime ends, the pup will want to take a nap or lie down. Bringing them to the room with the caged pet will allow them to associate the area with a calm feeling, and they won't be agitated by the other pet's presence (Hodgson, n.d.).

◆ Give your other pet lots of attention and care. You do not want your current pet to feel threatened by the new addition to the family. Feed them before the puppy, greet them first, and give them attention if they come up to you while you are interacting with the puppy. This will reinforce that they are still important to you, and the puppy has not taken you away from them (Hodgson, n.d.).

◆ When it's time to introduce your pet to a free-roaming animal like a cat, let the cat have control over the situation. Put the puppy in a den and let the cat walk around freely. Let your cat sniff and investigate the den. If the puppy is agitated, step in to calm them down, but don't shoo the cat/other pet away. Eventually, if the pets seem calm, you can let them meet face-to-face. It may be a good idea to have the puppy on a leash and have a toy ready to distract them if needed.

◆ Allow your pet to establish its boundaries. It is normal for a cat to swipe or growl at a puppy. Do not punish them for this. It is their way of establishing a personal bubble and feeling like they have control over the situation (Hodgson, n.d.).

When Should I Start Socialization?

The short answer is… right away!

But we need a few key rules to make this work. Before you introduce your puppy to anything new, such as people, other animals, different environments or sounds, you need to make sure to have your dog's attention. Start introducing things from a distance and work your way closer and closer to the actual item or person.

Let's say you want your dog to get familiar with horses. How you would go about that is to go to a country road somewhere where there are horses and train your puppy with a big enough distance between you and the horses. Then you gradually move closer and closer, but make sure the dog is still paying attention to you instead of this distraction. If they don't want to take food from you anymore, you should get more distance between you and the stimulus.

Basically, socialization means that your dog needs to get familiar with new things in a calm and controlled manner, without any insecurities or stress. In other words, the dog doesn't necessarily have to kiss the horse or touch the horse in any way to become socialized with horses. The process is more focused on desensitizing new things.

Getting your puppy familiar with different types of people is an important part of letting them adjust to their new life as a growing dog. The first few weeks are essential for you to help them understand what to expect out of unfamiliar humans. Have your friends come over to meet the puppy. Invite your friends in and take the puppy out for a training session inside your house while they are watching. Keep the attention on you and reward with a play session. These appointments should be fun, pleasant, and full of playtime, but you should keep them limited to short amounts of time. One or two guests at a time are enough, and large crowds should be avoided until your puppy is used to meeting strangers.

Let's move on to getting your puppy familiar with different environments. He might be able to sit and lie down on your carpet at home, but that doesn't mean he'll do it outside in the grass. Beaches, dirt roads, pavement, hard wooden floors are all examples of different environments for a dog. to tackle this you will train them in all of these environments to get them used to it.

By now you already know what I'm going to say. How do you socialize your puppy with things he doesn't know or sounds that are new? You guessed it, do some obedience training while unfamiliar sounds are blasting in the background. Train them around bikes, skateboards, the vacuum cleaner, etc. Keep their attention on you and the exercise, you'll notice after a while that they will become desensitized and in other words socialized with whatever's new a that moment in time.

When to Enroll in Puppy Classes?

If you want to sign up for training courses, this is the time to enroll. The first or second week of your training is the ideal time to get the puppy involved in a structured environment where they can practice the basics. Starting as early as possible will give you the maximum amount of time to train together with a professional.

CHAPTER TWO

Getting Familiar (weeks 9-10)

You did it. You got through the first week of puppy life! From here, everything is going to be just as challenging, but that's okay. The bond between you and your pup has been forged, and from here on out, they are looking to you for guidance. That bond will fuel the progress of training for the next seven weeks and deepen more along the way.

When a friend of mine, Charlotte, started training her new German Shepherd named Grover, she ran into a few bumps early on. Potty training, crate training, and everything else seemed to go okay initially, but before long, she realized something terrible. No matter what she did, Grover was absolutely terrified of everything. The door, the oven, the vacuum, and even his own reflection made him cringe. After a while, she found that Grover was so good in the crate because he simply didn't want to leave. She could only coax him out with food!

Eventually, Charlotte realized that Grover felt overwhelmed by everything being thrown at him in his first few weeks at home. She often had friends over

'My fashion philosophy is, if you're not covered in dog hair, your life is empty.'

- ELAYNE BOOSLER

and let all of them meet the puppy right away. She liked to talk on the phone, watch T.V., and do her chores in the same room as the puppy, which created a lot of noise when Grover wanted to sleep. Whenever someone came to the door, she would hide the puppy away to keep him from barking at the stranger. It made Grover think that people coming to the door was something to be afraid of.

Her puppy trainer advised her to work on socializing Grover with more people, but one at a time, so that he could get used to humans in a more stable environment. She also learned that she needed to spend time in the room doing things with Grover, instead of doing things he didn't understand while he was afraid. By week two, Grover was glad to come out of the crate and play with Charlotte's friends and family whenever they came over.

Here is a great example of the potential consequences you can find with an unsocialized puppy. Just because your pup is friendly with you in private doesn't mean they will be friendly with everyone. A lack of exposure to the world is more harmful than protective at the end of the day.

Weekly Goal

Week one was all about homecoming, setting rules, and making your puppy comfortable in the house. Now, we're going to work with those rules and turn a comfortable puppy into a productive puppy. This doesn't mean that the things you worked on in week one are done and gone.

Week Two Goal: Nurture the growth of your relationship with the puppy.

You need to continue practicing your leash training, potty training, socializing, and everything else from last week. Repetition is vital for your puppy to get the hang of things, and it is your job to reinforce that repetition through your routine training exercises.

Frequently Asked Questions

This week is all about taking the next step to solidify basic manners and house rules for your puppy to understand. During this period, you'll see the initial reactions your puppy has to what you have tried to train on so far. Barking too much in the crate, eating strange food, and destroying the furniture are just a few common responses the pup might have to learning new things. Don't feel discouraged if your puppy is having difficulties like this. Week two is all about reinforcing growth in the right direction and nurturing that comfort you showed your puppy during week one. It will establish trust between you and make it clear to your pup that your intentions are for the best.

So let's take a look at some of the questions you probably have at this point in training.

When Should I Start Teaching My Puppy Basic Obedience Exercises?

You can begin teaching these basics as soon as you think you're ready. You don't have to tackle every obedience exercise this week, though. Start with sitting, and move on to the rest when your puppy has that under control. Make sure to keep the training sessions short and sweet, 10 minutes at the maximum.

Let's take a look at a couple of exercises and how you can teach your puppy to do them. But remember, take your time and one exercise at a time!

Sit

1. Hold your treat above your puppy's head as a lure.

2. When your puppy moves backward, they will naturally sit down.

3. As soon as they sit, mark the behavior with a 'good sit!' and give them a treat.

4. Repeat a few times until they understand.

5. Remove the lure treat, and just use a closed hand to repeat Steps 1-4.

6. If your puppy sits down properly, just using your hand to lure, that means he's ready for you to mark it.

7. How? Start adding the word 'sit!' to your hand gesture.

8. When they sit, mark and reward the behavior with a treat. End the exercise by saying 'break', have a little play session, and let your buddy know he's done well.

Repeat this as much as you need to until your puppy gets the hang of it. If your puppy is doing well, you can remove the use of treats to use toys and praise as a reward instead. What you absolutely don't want to do, is force your puppy to sit by pushing them down.

The word 'break' is one that will become very important during training. It basically means that your puppy is free to do what they want to do and don't need to pay attention to you anymore. You ask them to do something, they do it, you release them with 'break'.

Stay

This exercise should only be taught when the 'sit' is a learned and confirmed behavior.

1. What's important for this exercise is that your puppy is leash trained. If not, then go back to chapter one, question 5.

2. Start by teaching a word for release. It can be 'go' or 'ok' or anything else you want, as long as it is consistent. I always use the word 'break' myself.

3. Get your puppy to sit, and throw a treat on the floor a few feet away from them.

4. When they go to get the treat, let them, but say the release word at the same time.

5. Repeat this a few times.

6. Start saying the release word without throwing a treat, and see if they get up anyway. If so, give the treat afterward. If not, throw the treat and say 'break' again.

7. Once they have the hang of this, start focusing on the 'stay' part by having them start in a sit.

8. While they sit, wait a few moments, and then reward them with your voice. Use the release word to let them go and throw a treat. Repeat this multiple times. In a later stage we will use distractions and duration to make this exercise more challenging for your puppy.

9. You don't actually need to mark this exercise with the word 'stay'. You can if you want to but it's not necessary. If you tell them to sit,

that in and of itself should tell them that they need to stay seated and can only be released when you say 'break'.

10. If the puppy gets up you say 'no' or 'eh eh'. If you have a very smart puppy they'll sit back down again. If they don't do that right away, just tell them to sit again.

11. For now, limit the length of this exercise (unless you feel your puppy is ready). At this age, your expectations should be limited to what the puppy is capable of. If they stay for a few seconds, that is good enough for now. You can work on duration and distance later.

An extra tip I want to share with you.. Use a blanket, your puppy's bed or anything else your dog can sit on to practice 'stay'. First start with the exercise explained above, so that your puppy understands the concept of staying in one place until you release them. Afterwards you can teach your dog the 'place' command.

'Place' means your dog has to go to their bed, the blanket or anything else and stay there. Imagine this.. You are enjoying a binge watching Sunday afternoon and somebody rings the doorbell. Your puppy will get up to meet the person at the door, something you want to prevent from happening. After much practice and lots of repetitions you will be able to ask your dog to go to his place and stay there, so you can open the door without any issues.

If you start them young, they will get the hang of it quickly. Be consistent, keep repeating and reward your dog when they stay on their bed like you've asked them to.

Look

Attentiveness is one of the keys to raising an obedient dog. If your dog is not paying attention to you, you might run into problems down the line like leash pulling, barking at other dogs, leash reactivity and much more.

1. Begin with a treat in your hand. Let your puppy sniff your hand, then lure them up to your face.

2. When they look at you, reward by giving them the treat.

3. After a few repetitions, add the command 'look' to the action. Start by saying it right when they look at you, then progress into saying it before you lure them with the treat.

4. When your pup gets the hang of this, remove the treat from your hand, but still gesture up to your face and say 'look.' If they follow the command, mark and reward with a treat from somewhere else or praise.

5. Repeat until your puppy is looking when you say 'look,' and wean the treats over time.

6. You can add this exercise during other parts of training once they get good at it. For instance, you can use the look command when a squirrel runs by and your dog wants to chase it. Make sure the reward is of higher value (something they love but don't get that often – either a toy or food) than the chase after the squirrel.

Lie Down

1. Use a similar luring method that you did to teach 'sit,' if it worked for your puppy.

2. Get your puppy to sit or stand in front of you, and lure them with a treat.

3. Bring the treat in a closed fist to the ground and hold it there until your puppy naturally lies down to sniff it.

   a. There are other ways to lure your puppy into a lying position if this doesn't work. Some people get down on the floor with the treat, moving towards the chest of the dog. It will get them to move backward and down to find it. You can also lure the puppy under a chair with the treat, which will convince them to get down.

4. Mark the behavior and reward with a treat.

5. Repeat this until your puppy starts to figure it out. Start pairing the action with your command, 'lie down.'

6. Over time, remove the lure treat, and just use your fist. You can still reward them after succeeding.

7. Eventually, you can replace the treat with another reward like playtime or praise and incorporate 'lie down' into longer training exercises with multiple steps.

Keep in mind that a lot of puppies have trouble with this exercise. If it doesn't work this week, try again next week and don't give up. But make sure to not push your puppy too much, they will learn eventually.

Good

I don't need to tell you much about the marker 'good'. The only thing you need to know is that you have to use it everytime your puppy does what you want him to do. Don't forget this step because it's a reinforcer of good behavior and a way for the puppy to learn they've done something right.

No

So, what happens if you're training your puppy and they do something they shouldn't? It's up to you to respond immediately and let your dog know that this specific behavior is not allowed. Mark it with the word 'no' or 'eh eh', but don't forget to REDIRECT them towards the behavior you do want.

You can put this in practice with a simple exercise like throwing a treat on the floor:

1. First step is to leash your puppy, especially when it's their first time trying this.

2. After that you ask your puppy to sit. You take a treat out, throw it on the floor and say 'no'. The idea is that the puppy will stay seated and look up at you.

3. Once he does that, give him your release command (break) and let him have the treat. Praise him with your voice as well.

4. Rinse and repeat.

Once you have this exercise down, you can move onto another. The word 'no' is a marker you'll use throughout their training and life. Remember to always use it when absolutely necessary to give it more impact when needed.

One last thing I want to share with you on obedience training. We are in week 1 now, but I don't want you to think that all of these exercises need to be taught during this week. I would suggest you starting in week 1 or 2 with these basic exercises, but it might take you a month or more to get the hang of it. Meaning that if your puppy only knows how to sit and look at you, that is okay. They all learn at a different pace and you should give them enough time to process everything. You can teach a dog to sit when they are 10 years old, so even though the first 8 weeks are crucial for your puppy, that doesn't mean you need to rush into things. So please, keep that in mind!

Heel

A dog that's is used to heeling and does a good job at it will become an amazing partner during your walks. If you are struggling with a dog that pulls on the leash, I suggest you take a good look at this exercise and start practicing it right away. Here's how you do it:

1. Have your dog on your left side to train this exercise and hold a treat in your left hand.

2. Step back with your left foot and lure your dog with your left hand back.

3. Then step forward again with your left foot and bring your left hand forward as well.

4. If all goes well, the dog will follow your hand and sit or stand next to you once you finish.

5. Always mark with 'good' and release the dog with 'break'.

6. Don't name the command yet because it's important to only start naming the command once you are confident you can get the behavior.

A little tip in between here: if your dog is not food motivated enough, use their actual food instead of treats. So you wouldn't feed them in the morning but rather do the feeding during training. This will get your puppy food motivated very quickly.

7. Repeat the exercise over and over until your puppy gets it. That's the moment you start marking it with 'heel'.

8. Repeat this exercise again multiple times but now only feed the dog on the release command and not the 'good' command anymore. That way you can phase out the lure.

Take your time with this exercise and remember this won't be a finished product immediately. If your dog doesn't get it right away, just keep practicing. For some dogs (and people) it might take weeks, for others days.

9. After your dog has this first part down, you can move onto walking a few steps forward.

10. Always step forward with your LEFT leg and don't name the behavior yet. If your dog follows your left leg, reward with 'good' and give a treat.

11. Repeat multiple times until you feel you can get the right behavior from your dog. That's when you do the same exercise of stepping forward again, but now you mark the behavior with 'heel'. Reward with 'good' everytime the dog follows.

12. Only start phasing out the treats when your dog is doing well with this exercise.

13. After that the only thing left to do is add distractions and different environments to the mix.

Never forget to always walk forward with your left leg instead of the right. I promise you, if you have a couple of 10-minute training sessions a day, you'll have a dog that won't pull on the leash, a dog that will look to you for guidance and a dog that you can show off to your friends.

Recall

There will come a time when your puppy is ready to walk off leash without you having to be scared they'll run away. This probably won't happen in the first week though, but you can work your way up. Creating a good recall is very important for your pup's safety as well as your sanity. Image your puppy off leash, having the time of their lives but all of a sudden they decide to bolt towards a very busy street. Every dog owners nightmare, right?! This is when your 'recall' comes in handy to avoid potentially dangerous situations.

So let's take a look at how you can teach your puppy to come back to you in every situation?

1. Your puppy needs to be leash trained in order to teach this exercise.

2. Take your pup outside to an open area without distractions.

3. Use a long leash.

4. Make sure your pup is watching you before going any further.

5. Get a couple of treats in one hand and throw them away from you, your puppy will run after them.

6. Once he has eaten the treats, call him back to you with the command 'come'. Use a little leash pressure.

7. When he runs to you, say 'good' and give him another treat.

8. Give your release command 'break' and throw a couple of treats away from you again. The dog will run after it and grab the treats. Then you call them back again, slight leash pressure if they don't come back right away.

9. Dog runs back to you, you say 'good' and reward again with a treat.

10. Rinse and repeat until your puppy starts doing it automatically.

11. Then you can move on to other environments with more distractions or use more distance between you and the dog.

These steps will condition your dog to become a pro at recalling. A little extra tip from me for those of you with dogs that are less food motivated, you can always use a toy or something else the dog loves. It could even be a little play session with you everytime they come back to you. Whatever motivates the dog is fine, so you'll have to think creatively.

My Puppy Barks and Whines Constantly in the Crate. How Can I Prevent This From Happening?

There are a few ways to tackle the problem of a puppy who does not want to be crated. Before you try to train on this behavior, ask yourself a few questions.

How long are you putting them in the crate? If they are constantly barking to be let out, first make sure you haven't let them stay in there for too long.

Secondly, **how much have you trained them on keeping the door shut?** Closing the door on the crate is an easily teachable topic, but it takes some work over time. When the door is closed, they may whine or bark when they want out. You don't want to make them feel unhappy for being locked in the crate, but you also do not want to reward this behavior. Don't open the door when the puppy is whining. Instead, wait until the puppy is calm, and then immediately open the door.

You will want to gradually lengthen the amount of time it takes for you to open the door after they whine. At first, you can open it after a few moments. Next time, make them wait a little longer. You also want to reinforce consistent times when the crate is always closed, with no exceptions (The Humane Society, 2018). Establishing this routine will solidify their expectations and help them understand the training.

If these things don't curb the barking, follow these steps to curb the behavior:

1. When you return inside, give them a toy or something else distracting in the crate. This will occupy their attention in the crate and remind them that it is a safe place to be.

2. When the dog is quiet, you can reward this behavior by letting them out for cuddles, playtime, or treats. It will show the pup that barking in the crate does not get a reward, but being good means that they might be let out for fun times.

The best way to keep them from barking in the crate is to introduce longer and longer periods inside. Continue the crate training practices you learned in Chapter 1.

A bedtime routine is also a great way to make sure you get the best experience during the first few weeks of long nights with your pup. By making a consistent routine of when you go to bed, and how that means it's time for the crate, your puppy will sync up its sleeping schedule with yours. At this age, puppies will need to be let out to pee every three to five hours, at least. It means you will likely have to get up and check on your puppy in the crate during the night. It isn't fun, but it will ensure that your puppy doesn't have accidents in the crate.

If your puppy has already gone to the bathroom, likes their crate, and still barks, there are a few things you can try to make them feel more at home in their bed.

◆   Pet your puppy until they fall asleep. If they like your attention, stay with them until they're relaxed. Resist the urge to do this in response to every bark, though, or they will learn that barking gets your approval. Wait until they are quiet, then pet them as a reward, and let them doze off.

    •   Make sure that you do not give in to the temptation to remove them from the crate during this time. Petting is okay, but it should be done in a position where you are reaching into the crate, not taking them out.

◆ If you need to sleep somewhere near the crate, like a couch, this is okay for the first few nights. Your puppy might be less nervous if they aren't entirely alone. Just make sure you wean them off the habit eventually so you can sleep in your own bed.

◆ Adding "white noise" like a ticking clock or a quiet T.V. might help to emulate the sounds your puppy was used to when sleeping with their litter. A quiet house can be scary, and barking is their way of making it clear they think it's TOO quiet.

◆ Exercise more during the day. If your puppy is barking a lot in their crate-time, it might be because they are still full of energy. By tiring them out during training, playtime, and other active parts of the day, you can make sure they are ready to sleep when you are.

At What Age Can My Puppy Stay Home Alone?

You can start now, but you need to make sure you take it slow. Leaving your puppy home alone should always be done one phase at a time. You need to be prepared to come home and check on your puppy during longer outings at first or have a pet-sitter ready to do the same. There are a few things you can do to ease them into the process in stages.

◆ Practice being alone. Before you ever actually leave the house, give your puppy some alone time in their crate or another safe, confined area. Give them a toy, then leave the room for a few minutes. When you return, reward them. Repeat this a few times, leaving for longer periods. Never return and reward if your puppy is barking or whining. Wait until they are calm, and then come back. If your puppy is content on its own, don't end the time early. Instead, quietly give them a treat, and then leave again to extend the alone time (Gibeault, 2019a).

- Some dogs might like the quiet noise of a television, radio, or music.

- When you leave the house, make sure it isn't for very long at first. If you can come back to check on the puppy, or have someone else do it for you, do so. It is essential for potty breaks, and will also ease the puppy more slowly into the idea of being left alone for a long time. Puppies should never be left alone for more than a few hours at a time.

- Don't be discouraged if the puppy can only last a few minutes without barking or whining. Some puppies learn this slower than others, and you will have to build up duration over time. Any progress is progress that should be rewarded.

Well, my lovely reader, I'm not going to sugarcoat it, this is usually a lengthy process with ups and downs. Start practicing this right away while you are present in the house, and have a gradual build-up. If you're getting frustrated, your puppy will be too. So leave the exercise for what it is and come back to it another time.

My Puppy Is Destroying the Furniture. How Do I Stop This?

A common problem that might start from day one is chewing. Puppies like to chew, especially at this stage in their life. Chewing relieves mouth pain and anxiety for these pups.

When it results in destroyed couches, chairs, carpets, etc., the first thing on your mind might be: *why?* So why do puppies chew? Sometimes it may be because they are teething or simply because they're nervous. Whatever the case may be, most puppies end up doing it when introduced to a new environment. This may be confused with biting if the puppy decides that your pants, legs, or arms are good chew toys.

61

Here are a few common reasons a puppy is chewing or destroying furniture.

- **Teething** - Your pup has new teeth, and their mouth hurts!

- **Exploring** - They're curious. Putting unfamiliar things in their mouth is a puppy's way of figuring out what they are.

- **Boredom** - Chewing can be a form of idle play if your pup doesn't have enough to do.

- **Hunger** - If your puppy isn't fed enough, they might be looking for food elsewhere.

- **Attention** - Your puppy might notice that you pay more attention to them or let them outside when they destroy things. This can make them believe that chewing is a way of asking to be let out or acknowledged.

- **Sickness** - This is not often the issue, but sometimes your puppy may be chewing because something is wrong. If you feel like your puppy may be distressed beyond the usual growing pains, talk to your vet (Hansen, 2018).

Fortunately, in most cases, this is a straight-forward problem to solve. It's also an excellent opportunity to introduce training techniques to you and your pup. From the beginning, you should have a variety of safe and appropriate chew toys to present to your puppy when they are chewing something. Keep them hidden away when they are not needed, so they are more interesting when they appear.

When you catch your puppy chewing something that is not a toy, say 'no!' or 'stop!' or whatever redirection word that you want to train them with. Remove them from the thing they are chewing, and put a chew toy in their mouth. This replacement will show them that chewing is okay, but only with certain objects.

Never punish your pup for destruction if you do not catch them in the act. Taking them to something they did three hours ago and yelling at them will not make sense to the puppy. You should also never pull them outside or give them food directly in response to destroying things. You might think you're punishing them by removing them from the problem, but in reality, you're showing them that chewing is a valid way of getting food, attention, or being let outside.

My Puppy Is Afraid of Everything. Why Is That and How Should I Handle It?

Between 8-16 weeks of age, socialization is one of the most important things for a puppy to experience. One of the most common problems with puppies is a lack of positive exposure to new humans, other animals, and strange environments. During the early periods of puppy development, they often experience a "critical fear period" (PetMD, 2019). This is when new elements of their life are most likely to be scary, and your job as their owner is to mitigate that fear.

Letting your puppy meet people that are tall, short, male, female, loud, soft, etc., will make it easier for them to interact with unfamiliar humans in the future. Some dogs develop fears of certain types of people if they haven't been properly socialized. Bringing various guests over can help them understand that all sorts of people exist, and humans are safe to be around.

You should still remember to take things easy. Baby steps are important to this process. At this stage, everything, and I mean *everything,* is new to the puppy. Things like carpet versus hardwood will be a big change, just like a public walk will be a lot different from an isolated stroll around the yard. If your puppy is afraid of people at first, roll things back, and try again when they're a little more comfortable in the home (Shojai, 2019).

If your puppy is still demonstrating anxious behavior, despite being friendly around people, you need to identify the fear before addressing the behavior. Some puppies are afraid of being alone, unfamiliar animals, children, or loud noises like footsteps or the television. Pay attention when your dog is exhibiting strange behavior, and take note of what happened to trigger it. Once you have a good idea of what it might be, you can follow these steps to tackle the fear.

1. Gauge the puppy's reaction. Every pup reacts to fear differently. Some might cower, hide, or retreat, while others may get aggressive, snap at the threat, or have an accident (Shojai, 2019). If they show strange behavior around a particular trigger, it might be a result of fear.

2. Continue to expose your pup to new things. New sounds, new people, new textures, etc., will make it clearer that changes in the puppy's environment do not need to be scary. These exposures should not be rushed. If he runs away from people, let him have his space and figure it out on his own schedule. These should be calm introductions, not forced.

3. If there is a particular trigger, try to eliminate it if possible. If not, expose your dog to it in small doses, and reward them if they remain calm. Pair the trigger with moments when they are relaxed (after eating, playtime) or when people are in the room.

4. Never reward your dog for acting scared. It may be counterintuitive, but don't cuddle, pet, or treat your pup when they exhibit signs of fear. It will teach them that it was a good thing to bark at the 'threat' of the T.V., and they will keep doing it. Instead, ignore their behavior until they calm down, and then reward them for being calm.

My Puppy Tries to Eat Everything He Comes Across. What Should I Do?

This is definitely a no-no. If your puppy feels free to eat anything they please, they are more likely to eat something that is unhealthy, poisonous, or a choking hazard. Setting boundaries during early training will make it clear that your pup is not supposed to eat anything other than dog food and treats.

Later on, this can become more distracting for your puppy if left unchecked. When on walks, playing at the park, or wandering the house, they need to know that eating strange objects is not safe. You never know what a dog might find out in the open, especially once they are out of puppy training. Establish these rules to ensure that your puppy knows not to be distracted by food and other tempting treats.

◆ Begging is unacceptable. Human food is off-limits, especially when it is on the table. To communicate this to the puppy, you can start off by never caving. Don't give them any "one-time" scraps from the table; they aren't healthy and it rewards them for begging.

• To train your puppy out of begging, you can teach them to stay in their bed or crate during dinner. Start off by

65

giving them a chew toy or a treat-filled toy on their bed or in their crate while you eat. Pair this with a 'lie down' or 'bed up' command. This will keep their attention and reward them for being in the right spot during this time. Until your puppy knows how to stay on the bed on its own, close the door so there is no chance of failure. Over time, you can remove the treats and just call them to their bed during dinner.

- Practice distraction training with your dog. This means training them to know there is a distracting item available to them but look to you for approval on whether or not it is okay for them to approach it.

  - To train your puppy on distractions, you can follow a few simple steps. First, place an appealing item on the ground a few feet from your dog. This can be a toy, treat, etc. Ask your dog to 'leave it,' and after a few seconds, give them a treat and remove the item. Repeat this training, lengthening the amount of time that the dog has to stay before getting a treat.

  - When you go on walks, keep up the same training. If your dog wants to sniff a tree or follow a squirrel, reinforce 'leave it' and give them a treat if they look to you before acting on their urges.

  - For bigger distractions, you can scale your rewards to match. If your dog looks to you before eating an abandoned hamburger bun on the table, give them a big piece of chicken or an extra-fun play session as a reward. This will train them that ignoring the food is always better than the satisfaction of stealing it.

My Puppy Chases My Kids. How Should I Handle It?

Children are naturally interesting to puppies. Some pups get along fine with kids, but some are more afraid of them. They move in ways that seem erratic, confusing, and scary to a puppy's perspective. In some cases, your puppy might think they are being playful when your kids are actually terrified by the dog running after them. It doesn't mean that they won't ever get along, but for a young pup still getting used to the world, children can be more difficult to get used to than adults.

Here are a few steps to try and teach your puppy it's not okay to run after the little ones.

1. **Train your kids first.** It means teaching them the puppy zone rules: no chasing the pup, no encouraging them to chase on purpose, no touching the puppy when sleeping, and no rowdy play that might scare them. Children need to know how to act around the puppy and play in a way that dogs understand.

2. **Teach your puppy 'down' or 'come.'** Training on these commands with high-value treats will make it easier for them to understand the words in more chaotic situations, like kids running around and playing.

   a. You can practice this by leading the puppy 'down' to the ground or to 'come' over to you with a treat. Make them hold the position for a moment, then mark and reward. Repeat this during your training sessions even after you think they understand it.

3. **Be consistent.** If your puppy jumps up on a kid, tell them 'down' even if the child is okay with the dog. The rule should be no chasing, no jumping, no exceptions.

4. **Let your kids be a part of the training.** Your dog will be less afraid or fascinated by children the more they see them. If your pup sees your children more often, they won't be as interested in chasing them around every time (Miller, 2010). They can also give the dog their dinner by putting the bowl down. Make sure you have the puppy wait until the children are out of the way before eating, so they do not lash out to protect the food.

How Do I Make My Puppy Less Scared of the Vacuum Cleaner?

Vacuums are one of the most common enemies of dogs, no matter what age. There is a reasonable explanation for this: vacuums are loud and smell weird! Puppies have sensitive ears, and they use smell as one of their primary sources of navigating the world, so this has a bigger impact than you might expect. It can result in barking, hiding, and chasing the vacuum, among other things.

So how can you help your pup understand that this stinky, noisy thing won't hurt them? Like always, there are a few simple solutions you can try.

◆ **Separate them.** Most obviously, you can move your puppy to another room, or outside when vacuuming. Being out of harm's way might be all you need to keep the pup from having a bad time. Of course, this isn't always possible in every situation.

◆ **Get them used to it.** Desensitization is a healthy way of exposing your puppy to a problem, slowly, over time, until they have learned that it isn't a threat. You can do this with a series of steps (Jones, 2019):

1. Start by getting the vacuum out and then putting it away in front of your pup. Don't vacuum yet. Just get it out and put it away.

2. Get the vacuum out and move it around without turning it on.

3. Get the vacuum out and turn it on in another room, where your puppy can hear it but doesn't have access to it.

4. Get the vacuum out and turn it on in the same room as your puppy for just a few minutes.

5. Repeat Step 4 for longer and longer periods of time.

6. Reward your puppy for being calm during any of these steps.

7. You can also try to play vacuum noises on a T.V. or computer during the day if you don't want to haul the vacuum out every time.

◆ **Try counter-conditioning.** This can be a separate process or done at the same time as desensitization. Counter-conditioning works by having your puppy associate vacuum time with something good, making them forget about the scary parts of it. You can do this by pairing vacuuming with getting a high-value treat, toy, or another incentive. Whatever the reward, make sure it is unique to vacuum time. It will make your puppy look forward to the vacuum since it means they get something special (Jones, 2019). Over time, this reduces anxiety associated with the event.

My Puppy Doesn't Like to Play With Any Toys. How Do I Teach This?

Playtime is important, and not just because it's cute to watch. Puppies who regularly play with toys are more mentally stimulated, burn energy in a healthier way, have a stronger bond with their owners, and have a higher quality of life. Play is also a great way of rewarding puppies during training and helps them learn skills more easily (Bender, 2019). If your pup isn't interested in toys yet, you should try and make them more appealing.

Some pups have a harder time learning to play because of poor socialization, or because their playful instincts lead them into more problematic games like chasing and hiding (Bender, 2019). Training on socialization and getting them used to people will always improve your pup's relationship with playtime.

When that isn't enough, here are a few ways you can make toys and play-time more intriguing for your puppy.

- **Be involved.** Giving your pup a toy and leaving them alone isn't going to make it seem very interesting. Engage with your puppy by playing tug of war, throwing the toy, or running around with them while they play. This will make it more of an engaging, social experience.

- **Reward playfulness…** no matter how small! If your puppy sniffs a toy, reward them with petting and a treat. Fill a toy with pea-nut-butter or hide a treat near it. If they play with a toy on their own, mark and reward that behavior. This will get them started on checking out the toy, and then they will learn that the toy itself is fun too.

- **Add games to training.** Using toys and playtime as a reward during training, or as a training exercise is a great way to show your puppy what it is good for. Some dogs understand learning better than playing. Teaching the step-by-step process of playing fetch will show them the game in a way that is good for their brains and for developing a relationship with play (Bender, 2019).

- **Trust your dog's interests.** Observe your puppy and see what they like. Believe it or not, they have opinions of their own. Your pup might not care for ropes and tug-of-war, but bouncing balls are a whole different story! Breed and personality can play into what kind of games your puppy likes. Go with what they are naturally interested in, and don't be afraid to try a wide variety of toys.

Why Is My Puppy Eating Their Own Poop? How Do I Handle It?

The scientific name for this problem is coprophagia, and it is more common than you might think. There are a few different steps you can take to eliminate the behavior once and for all.

1. **Eliminate the temptation.** This means making sure there are not a lot of opportunities for your puppy to eat feces. Yes, I'm talking about cleaning up the yard. Picking up your puppy's poop right away is a great way of making sure they will stop doing it. If they repeatedly want to eat poop and there is no poop to be eaten, they will eventually forget the habit.

2. **Change their diet.** If necessary, you can add certain things to your puppy's food that will change the smell of their poop and the enzymes in their belly. In some cases, this can make them less interested in eating feces. Shredded zucchini and grated pineapple are safe recommendations for this (Simpawtico Training, 2017). You can also ask your vet for medications that you can put in the dog's food for the same effect.

3. **Revisit potty training.** Even if your puppy is only going outside, they might still have some anxiety about the process. Go back to giving your pup a treat immediately after going potty. This will reinforce potty training and interrupt the 'instinct' they have to eat feces (Simpawtico Training, 2017). It will help curb the habit and give you time to pick up the poop.

4. **Use 'leave it.'** Practicing this command gives you an easy tool to use in the case of a coprophagic puppy. If they have started to understand 'leave it' from your training sessions, this is an excellent opportunity to use it. Give them the command, and reward the puppy if they succeed.

5. **Distract them.** Some trainers recommend distributing dry food or other healthy, non-treat snacks around the yard. This will give your puppy something else to sniff and hunt down when they're bored and keep them from reinforcing the bad habit of eating poop.

Puppies that eat their own poop may do so for a couple of different reasons. Once you think you know the reason behind your puppy's habit, you might have an easier time training them out of it.

◆ **Cleaning up/Hiding** - They may have been punished for bathroom accidents too harshly in the past, or have another reason to be ashamed of going potty. As a result, they might be eating the poop to get rid of it and not be caught (Simpawtico Training, 2017).

◆ **Hunger/Anxiety** - If a dog has a history of hunger, homelessness, or stress, it might have formed a habit of eating poop. In times of desperation, some dogs form the habit, and it's hard to unlearn after they have a healthy home.

◆ **Boredom/Curiosity** - Some pups are just interested in poop. It smells interesting, it's small enough to eat... so why not? It usually results in eating poop from another animal or has been in the yard a long time.

◆ **Sickness** - This is less common, but sometimes coprophagia is a symptom of a nutrient deficiency in the body. If your puppy isn't getting something they need, they may instinctively eat their poop to retain some form of sustenance (Simpawtico Training, 2017). Ask your vet about this if you feel like this behavior is not going away or your dog has other health issues.

CHAPTER THREE

Expanding Horizons (weeks 10-11)

By week three, you have probably had some successes and challenges alike with your puppy. That is totally normal, and it means there is a lot of room for training in the weeks to come.

When my friend Ken started training his dog Bella, things went great at first. She picked up sitting, lying down, and all the other basics pretty quickly. Ken thought things would be easy by week three, but that's when he got a little surprise...

He had used the same bag of treats that he kept on a counter in the kitchen, through all of his training. Bella loved treats and would be eager to begin training when she knew it would come with her favorite snacks. Because of this, she was always well-behaved during training. That's when she started to get clever.

It started around the holidays when Ken started getting packages at the door on a daily basis. When the doorbell rang, Bella would go absolutely crazy, barking and running towards the door. To keep her

'A dog will teach you unconditional love. If you can have that in your life, things won't be too bad.'

- ROBERT WAGNER

from freaking out the delivery man, Ken would give her a treat in the kitchen and then go to the door while eating it. This got her to stop running to the door and going crazy, but it spawned a new problem.

Now, whenever the doorbell rang, if Ken didn't give her a treat, Bella would find her way up onto the counter to sniff one out herself. She figured out where they came from, of course, but she only wanted to steal them when the doorbell rang. It turns out that she had begun to associate someone coming to the door with getting a treat, and it always allowed her to be alone with them when Ken went to the door! Even after he moved the treats somewhere else, she would bark and bark and run around the house every time the doorbell rang. Somehow, he had made things worse.

Weekly Goal

Week three is when your puppy has started to get comfortable in the house. They're getting the hang of their new home, and they're getting smarter all the time. This is great for picking up new skills and training, but it also means that they might get too smart for their own good. A clever puppy will find ways to get into trouble, whether it's for the sake of mischief or curiosity.

Week Three Goal: Establish the expectations and boundaries of different situations.

For your training this week, focus on making your expectations of good behavior clear to your puppy. They might be learning fast or still working on some of the basics, but at this stage, they are able to understand your cues. Your puppy will be able to tell the difference between you being happy or disappointed in their behavior and adjust accordingly. This week is all about establishing a pattern of good behavior that your pup can apply to different places and activities in the future.

Frequently Asked Questions

Even as you try new exercises, at this stage you should still be repeating what you've already learned in earlier weeks. Practice makes perfect, and that goes double for puppies. Keep training on the same things you've learned in weeks one and two. If your puppy is learning fast and is eager for more, add the old tricks to sessions where they are learning something new. Have them sit before leash training or stay in one place before going on to the next step of a session. You can integrate the basics into future sessions to give your pup that repetition while mixing it up and keeping it exciting.

Let's have a look at 'the art of attention' before we move on to new topics. I think the time has come to start working on this exercise.

Puppies are usually all over the place, busy with discovering the world, sticking their noses where they don't belong, and pretty much doing everything they shouldn't be doing. This is all very normal behavior but you want the process of paying attention to you to start as quickly as you can.

The art of attention doesn't necessarily mean the dog needs to look at you, it involves much more than that. In a world of distractions, they will learn that the only thing they need to do is look for your guidance and follow along. If you do it well, it will reinforce the bond you have with your dog immensely. The idea is that your dog will start to enjoy ignoring all of what's happening around him.

So how do we get the dog's attention?

1. You can only do this exercise once your dog knows his markers (sit, look, break, good and no).

2. Start using your dog's actual food (the food that you would normally give in a bowl). Stopping bowl-feeding will ignite attention right away.

3. Your dog needs to know right from wrong to be able to do this attention exercise. So use the markers you taught hem: good, no, break.

4. Lots of repetition to get this right, paired with the right leadership will bring you success.

5. Work on it on a daily basis. Consistency is key!

6. So let's take a look at a simple example:

   a. Make your dog sit on his bed/a towel or anything else you want to use. Basically ask him to 'place'.

   b. Stand in front of him and give him the 'look' command. If he looks into your eyes, lock that in and keep him there.

c. Release with 'break' and reward.

d. After a while you can work on duration and distractions. Have somebody walk around your dog while you are asking them to look at you for example. Your dog will need trust in you to not look at the other person.

e. The end product will be a dog that keeps his eyes on you at all times, literally and figuratively, and will more than likely not suffer or suffer less from any behavioral problems down the line.

Grabbing your dog's attention will serve you in every aspect of your dog's training and life in general. So my advice is to train on a regular basis to get the foundation as strong as it can be. You'll thank me later!

When Can I Start Walking My Puppy on a Leash?

This is a complicated question. It's fine to take your puppy out on short walks outside during this time, and it's actually a great way to start leash training early. You need to keep in mind that young puppies are not completely vaccinated yet at this age. Taking your dog to a popular trail, dog park, or anywhere else where they might meet other animals is risky. You don't want them to catch diseases they are not protected against yet, especially if they aren't adequately trained on avoiding other dogs when on-leash.

If you do decide to take them somewhere where there are other dogs, like someone else's home, make sure those dogs are vaccinated. I still would not recommend doing this. Instead, I would recommend going to a parking lot or somewhere paved, where you are unlikely to find other dogs. In this environment, you can train on the leash or practice exercises like sit and stay. If other dogs approach, do not let them sniff each other and prevent your puppy from eating anything unfamiliar on the ground.

I typically teach leash skills and walking etiquette when puppies are 14-15 weeks old, so week seven of this guide will cover it in more detail. At that time, the pup is fully vaccinated and more mature. If you think your puppy is ready for leash training now, skip ahead to that chapter for instructions.

How Do I Settle Down a Rowdy Puppy?

If your puppy tends to get over-excited or active during certain parts of the day, it can be a struggle to focus on training, work, cleaning, or whatever else you may be doing at the time. Luckily, this is a trainable issue. You can teach 'settle down' as a command, or something more direct, like 'bed up' or 'go to your place.' These commands are used to tell your puppy it's time to calm down and associate it with leaving the area that is causing all the ruckus.

Here are a few steps to teach this command to your puppy and make it easier for them to chill out in an active environment. When you introduce this technique, start in a quiet training area, without any distractions (Stil-well, n.d.). Later on, you can practice it with more people in the room to simulate a real situation.

1. Have your dog sit or stand still and step a short distance away from them.

2. With a treat in hand, lure them to their bed, crate, or another area you want to designate as their 'place.'

3. Once they follow the lure, say 'go to your bed!' or whatever phrase you want to use. Keep it consistent.

4. When they are on the spot, whether they sit or not, give them the treat.

5. Repeat this a few times. When they start to get the hang of it, make them sit or lie down before giving a treat. Feel free to add additional rewards like praise or pets, but do not get them rowdy with active play as a reward.

6. Next, remove the lure treat entirely, and just use your hand. Repeat a few times, and reward only once the puppy is lying in their spot.

7. Increase the amount of time they have to lie in the spot before giving a reward, and decrease the amount you have to lure him with your hand. Over time, you can graduate to pointing at the area, and giving the command.

8. Keep practicing this with more distance between you and the spot, and longer times spent there before receiving a reward.

How Do I Build Confidence in My Puppy?

Training is always going to be an uphill battle. If you find that your puppy is nervous, unsure, or hesitant during training, it might be because they aren't confident in what they are doing. You can combat this by bringing patience to every training session and letting your puppy advance at their own pace. If something takes a little longer to learn, do not give up. Continue repeating it and rewarding your puppy when they make progress, even if it is just the smallest step forward.

Some of the tools you have already used in weeks one and two can be wielded to boost confidence in your puppy. Here are a few techniques you can integrate into your training to make your puppy feel calmer, more capable, and overall more confident in their behavior.

- ◆ **Desensitization** - Small, unexpected things can make your puppy less comfortable in specific environments. Identifying triggers like certain noises, smells, people, actions, or objects can help you realize where to focus desensitization training for your puppy. Revisit the tips in Chapter 2 if you want to try desensitization with a source of stress for your puppy.

- ◆ **Counter-conditioning** - By creating positive associations, you can get your puppy used to anything. You learned about this technique when we discussed vacuums in week two. This same technique can be used to make your puppy feel more confident in puppy class, in the car, on a leash, or in any other unfamiliar situation.

- ◆ **Enrichment** - You can use a number of tools to help make your puppy feel a little smarter while living their life outside of training. There are food bowls, toys, and treat dispensers designed to make dogs solve a small puzzle before getting a reward for themselves. Investing in these types of enrichment objects for your pet can let them put their natural hunting, tracking, problem-solving skills to use in the house.

- ◆ **Socialization** - A pet that struggles with socialization at this stage will feel less confident on its feet at any given time. Don't stop socializing your pup just because you haven't seen them bite anyone yet. There's more to it than that.

How Do I Introduce the Car?

Introducing the car, like anything else with a new puppy, is a multi-staged process. You will want to teach your pup about the car one piece at a time, depending on how interested they are and how anxious it makes them. Here is a quick guide to getting your puppy ready to drive around with you.

1. Bring them outside on a leash to investigate the car with all of the doors open. Let them sniff, and climb inside on their own if they want to. No driving yet, just checking it out.

2. Once your puppy is interested, throw a treat or a toy inside, and let them go after it. If you need to pick them up and put them in, do it gently, and don't force them to stay inside if they want out.

3. When the puppy is comfortable sitting in the car, give them another treat, and let them stay in the vehicle with a chew toy if they want to.

4. After a little while, coax them out of the car, and reward them once they get out.

5. Repeat these steps a few times, on different days if necessary, until your puppy is comfortable getting in, sitting, and getting out of the car.

6. You can introduce shutting the doors next, with you sitting in the front seat. If they are okay with this, turn the car on, and let them spend some time in the car while the engine is running. The sounds and smells of this might scare your puppy, so be ready to practice this step a few times.

7. Once your puppy is comfortable sitting in the car with their puppy harness or crate installed, you can try to drive around. Start with short drives around the block, and lengthen the drives over time.

8. At the end of every drive, mark and reward your puppy once they get out of the car.

My Dog Jumps Up at Everyone He Meets. How Do I Avoid This?

Revisit your training in previous chapters. You have several tools already to combat this behavior over time. If your dog has been working on 'settle down' or 'sit,' use those as a command before your dog starts to jump on someone. When someone new comes to the house, reward them for staying calm if your puppy doesn't jump.

You can also teach this behavior by providing treats on the floor when a new person arrives. This will get them in the habit of focusing on the floor, instead of up high, when someone is approaching. You can pair the treats with 'stay' or 'down,' if you want, and use that command later as you phase out treats. There are a few other rules that you can create to keep the puppy from being rewarded for jumping around and being crazy.

♦ Have your guests ignore the dog as much as possible when they jump. If you have to move them onto the floor, do not scold or pay attention to the dog after that. They want attention, so by ignoring them, you are teaching them that you do not think jumping on people is fun.

♦ Replace the behavior with something else. You can do this by establishing a pattern. When someone new comes in, immediately tell your dog to go to their bed or anything else they already understand. Keep this consistent, and they will start to form the habit of going to their bed every time someone new arrives. This will turn into their new greeting instead of jumping (Gibeault, 2020b).

♦ Another way of preventing the dog from jumping up at you is making them sit every time they approach you or someone else. This way he'll learn that people means sit.

- If you are about to embark on this jumping journey with your puppy, make sure to tire them out first. This will make it much easier for you to handle them and teach them the rules.

- As you've probably read through the lines, it's very important to use the leash for this exercise. Otherwise you have absolutely no control over the dog. You can either have your puppy wearing the leash right away when they exit the crate, or hang a leash on the front door. That way, you'll have access to it once a surprise guest visits.

Now let's focus on you, because your puppy might try to jump on you as well. Maybe in the morning when you come downstairs after a good night sleep and you let them out of the crate. Puppy is excited to see you and wants to greet you, but forgets the rules. Follow the steps like I taught you and you will have success.

How Can I Get My Dog Comfortable With Being Handled by Strangers?

Going to the vet, meeting guests, and walking at the park are all everyday situations where your puppy might be picked up, pet, and prodded by strangers. Eventually, most puppies like being handled by others, because cuddles and attention are fun. At first, some pups can be scared by all of this unfamiliar touching and react in harmful ways. This can present as growling, retreating, and biting. To prevent this, you can teach your dog to get used to handling throughout the day and during training sessions.

No matter what, make sure you step in if your dog seems too uncomfortable. Not every dog adapts to handling right away, and if your puppy is scared, don't prolong the experience. Think through what you are doing, and make sure the experience is fun for the pup. You should never have too many people surrounding them at one time, and the environment should be calm.

- Don't be shy at home. When petting, training, and playing with your puppy, get them used to the ins and outs of being handled by humans. Make sure you are regularly touching their ears, nose, eyes, toes, tail, tummy, and chin. This form of desensitization will get your puppy used to these feelings in a safe environment.

- Do handling training. This should be during your regular training sessions. One by one, give your puppy a little massage, imitating the pacing of a vet examination. One by one, touch and look at their ears, paws, inside the mouth, etc., and give him a treat between each part. It should be slow, and your puppy should be well-behaved and calm to get the treat.

- Let other family members and friends do this as well, in shorter bursts. As part of socialization, you can let friendly faces look in the puppy's ears, pet their belly, pick up their paws, etc., as long as they are gentle. Give the pup a treat for cooperating.

Ruff Ruff Recap (weeks 11-12 = 1 Month Goal)

Congratulations! You have had your puppy in training for one entire month. That means that you are halfway through this training plan, and you've done a lot of work to get here. The most important thing at this stage in your puppy's development is sustaining the exercises you've introduced and practicing what you have already learned. Instead of adding more new activities to the routine at this phase, it is more productive to use this week to focus on repetition and practice.

For this reason, this chapter will go over what you have learned so far during your training plan and recap the areas that you should be working on the most. If there are any areas that you have been neglecting, either because your pup seems to have figured them out already, or because they are a little exhausting, you should make sure to fit them in every day this week. Even one week without practicing a new behavior can be detrimental for a puppy, and make it harder to catch up with what they had once mastered.

'Dogs are not our whole life, but they make our lives whole.'

- ROGER CARAS

As an example, I think of my dog Reece. When we first started training, there were some things he picked up quickly and some things we needed to work harder on. After three weeks of 'leave it' training, I was pretty tired of it. I decided that he knew how to leave it and stopped working on it in favor of more impressive tricks.

It only took a week or so for Reece to forget his 'leave it' training altogether. I didn't notice at first, because we had stopped working on it, but it became relevant when we began leash training. Out on a walk, Reece happened across some litter that was full of old food. I have no idea how old it was or where it was from. Obviously, I didn't want him to eat it, so when he approached, I said, 'leave it, Reece,' expecting him to demonstrate his excellent behavior from weeks two and three. Well... he didn't!

Instead, he looked at me, and looked at the food, looked back at me, and... you can imagine what happened next. A feast of trash that only a wild puppy can appreciate was devoured. Luckily, he didn't manage to eat enough of whatever it was to get sick, but I was not thrilled about it regardless. He had understood 'leave it' time and time again, but since we hadn't practiced, he thought it wasn't a rule anymore.

In response, I made sure we re-trained everything we learned for the rest of the week instead of introducing anything new. I knew that Reece wasn't being lazy or forgetting what he'd learned so quickly. Because he had been so excited to learn new tricks, I had rushed us into more and more exciting exercises. I learned from this that an overwhelmed puppy isn't always stressed or upset by falling behind. It can happen because both human and dog are moving too quickly and not noticing what still needs practice.

Weekly Goal

This week's goal sounds simple, but it is important nonetheless. Repetitive practice is fun for a puppy, but it can be exhausting for a human in some cases. If you're getting tired of doing the same old commands every day, that is normal, but resist the urge to give in to it. When puppy training gets less interesting for you, it gets less interesting for your puppy too. They can tell when your enthusiasm is draining. That's why this week's goal is to find new ways to spice up your training sessions while still getting in that repetition.

Week Four Goal: Recap what you've learned, but spice it up!

It might sound challenging to bring a new perspective to training while keeping things consistent for your puppy. Don't worry. It isn't as hard as it seems. There are many ways to put a new spin on an old trick without changing the exercises' important parts. Here are a few ways you can add a little something extra to your training sessions that will make it seem new, while still retaining what you've already done.

- Expand your area.

- Try a new toy.

- Let someone else help.

Recap

For the rest of this chapter, we're going to go over everything we've learned so far, with some quick reminders about common issues you might be facing. If you have any questions, review FAQs from previous chapters, or flip ahead to see if we train further on it in the future.

You can also use this section as a checklist. This week, every day, try to train on all of these topics at least once with your puppy. If you miss one on one day, make sure you get it the next.

Rules of the House

If you made rules that were important to you during week one, take a look at them now. How many of these rules are you enforcing? Have you started to get lenient on any of them simply because your puppy hasn't caught on yet? This is normal, but now is a great time to revisit those rules and bring them back to the top of the list. You do not need to compromise on your boundaries for your puppy. Take this week to go through the rules again and make sure you train all of them.

Socializing With Humans

You may have noticed, but socialization is relevant for almost every standard puppy behavior you will encounter at an early stage. If your pup is doing anything strange around people in your house or out in public, it is likely that they are not yet fully socialized. Continue easing your puppy into different people, places, textures, sounds, and experiences. When you're on a walk, it's alright to let a neighbor pet your puppy, so long as you think the situation is calm enough. Little things like this will solidify your pup's relationship with the world and make everything new less scary in the long-run.

Socializing With Other Pets

If you have other dogs, cats, etc., they've likely had a chance to meet your puppy by now. Some animals catch on with each other sooner than others, so you may have fast friends or bitter rivals at this stage. No matter what, keep up that slow exposure to one another. Let your pets do things together with your observation, but give them the chance to act independently. It might mean playing with different toys in the same room, eating near each other, or sleeping on the same pillow. Not every dog will be okay with these things right away, so keep this in mind. Remember that the strategies we reviewed in week one can be used for as long as you need to.

Crate Training

At this stage, you probably know your puppy's opinions on the crate. Some pups catch on quickly and learn to love their den from the start. Others may be barking and whining still, at four weeks. Continue your training, either way. If your puppy is happy to go into the crate and stay inside all night, you can wean treats from the process, but you should still reward them for a job well done. Praise your puppy for going in the crate and make sure it is still a fun environment. New toys can show up in the crate to keep it appealing, and clean blankets are always more welcome than dirty ones.

If your puppy is struggling with the crate, try to tackle it from a new point of view. Is there something you can change about the crate to make it more of a den for your puppy? Remember, three sides of the crate should be covered, to create a more cave-like environment for the den. Check on your crate structure and see if any parts of it might be uncomfortable or cold at night. In some cases, you might have better luck with crate training if you change the time of day you focus on it. After eating, playing, walking, or other tiring activities, you can open up the crate and lure your puppy inside with the same steps as always. Since they're all tuckered out, it might be easier for them to fall asleep in the comfy den, and make that association with safety.

Potty Training

Whether you're still dealing with accidents or not, you should still be keeping to your potty training routine. Teaching your puppy a schedule is the best way to ensure that they stick to it in the long run, even if it hasn't kicked in yet. Puppies pee and poo more than adult dogs, so you will have to work with their schedule for the time being. Many puppies are starting to understand these boundaries at four weeks, but that doesn't mean they have them mastered. Remember my experience with Nalu. Even though it took seven months, she eventually got the hang of it, and now she is a potty master.

Leash Training

At four weeks, you can introduce your puppy to the early stages of behaving on the leash. Putting it on their collar, using it around the yard, and keep it on for some of your training exercises. Having the leash on while working on things like 'sit,' 'leave it,' and 'stay' will make it easier for them to understand that those commands are part of long walks too. Avoid taking your puppy out on a leash to anywhere that there might be strange dogs or animals, though. Remember, they aren't fully vaccinated yet, so this can be risky.

Chewing and Destruction

By four weeks, some of your chew toys might look a little rough. If your puppy needs some new things to chew on, don't be hesitant to replace them. Having a wide variety of fresh options will keep your puppy's mouth on the right things and away from your furniture and ankles. Keep using them as a replacement if you find them chewing anything else, and never punish your puppy for damage that you did not catch in the moment.

Car

At this age, you might be taking your puppy to classes, vet appointments, and longer trips around town. It's a great time to work on your car training. Instead of getting your puppy in right away when you need to take them somewhere, set out some extra time to work on the routine. Let them practice getting in and out of the car a few times before you hook them in and go. Even if they're already good at it, this repetition will solidify the routine and make it less scary.

Settling Down

This is an important command to keep practicing. Your puppy is going to be excited by all sorts of things, all the time. It won't change for a few years, even after they are well trained. Establish your key phrase and stick to it. One way to rehearse the 'settle down' command is to use it at the end of every training session. When you're done with your exercises for the day, practice 'settle down' a few times with lures and treats. End the session after your pup has successfully settled, and then give them some time to cool down in their place.

Proper Puppy Manners (weeks 12-13)

You are officially over the hump, and it's time to start the second month of puppy training. Now that you have some basics figured out, you can build upon them to push each puppy skill to the next level. This week will focus on the problems most pups face at 12-13 weeks old. This period is crucial to a dog's development because they are going through many significant changes in their bodies and minds.

At 12 weeks, my colleague Diane ran into a few unexpected issues with her puppy, Rex. He was great at understanding rules, boundaries, and limits for the most part. The crate was no problem, the yard was understood, everything was in order when it came to the usual puppy business. That's why it came as a surprise when Rex suddenly started behaving aggressively around the crate.

The emphasis here is on 'around.' He was fine going in the crate at night, behaved well inside, and never had any accidents. Still, whenever anyone in the family besides Diane approached the area, he would start

'The more boys I meet, the more I love my dog.'

- CARRIE UNDERWOOD

snarling and hunching down in front of it. It was completely unlike him, and it seemed like Rex was trying to guard the crate from anyone passing by.

This was strange, but Diane dismissed it since no one needed to go near Rex's crate most of the time anyway. If he was protective over his spot, that was alright with her. The problem is that when Diane allowed this behavior around the crate, Rex realized it was effective. He learned that if he hunched down and guarded things that were his, he could scare off anyone that might 'steal' it from him. He started growling when people walked near his food, or if someone besides Diane picked up his favorite toys. As you can imagine, what began as a non-issue became a huge problem. This little puppy had some big ideas about what was 'his' around the house.

Diane managed to get this behavior under control with some training on resource guarding. We'll go over that in more detail in this chapter because it's a common issue in puppies this age. Around one to two months, pups start to learn that this is their territory, leading to some worries about that territory being taken away from them. Don't worry. You won't have to remove your puppy's favorite blanket, toy, etc., from the picture entirely. Rex's beloved crate is still totally intact to this day. He just doesn't mind if someone else comes to get a look at it too.

Weekly Goal

During this week, you can narrow your focus to a few specific things. You should still be practicing your basic exercises every day, and gradually introducing things like long car rides, better potty training, and more extended periods alone at home. This is all just as important as it was last week and the week before.

Week Five Goal: Develop proper puppy etiquette and good manners.

As your puppy gets a little smarter, you can expand your horizons to start working on being a polite pup. Making messes, being selfish, and invading your space are all no-no's, and a spunky 12-week old pup will need to be reminded of that time and time again.

Frequently Asked Questions

We'll talk about some of the most common behavior issues to crop up around this time as examples. If you're running into any unique problems, feel free to experiment with these solutions anyway and adapt them to your puppy's situation. The framework of luring, capturing, redirecting, and positive reinforcement can be applied to many different behaviors in similar ways.

Teething Is in Full Swing, What Do I Do?

Teething is a big deal. Every pup is bound to deal with it differently, but teething problems can last as long as six months in some cases. Mouth pain/irritation is expected during this time and leads to problematic behaviors as your pal tries to relieve the pain in their own way. Chewing, biting, and rubbing their mouth on the furniture might seem like a messy hassle, but it is usually a sign that your puppy's teeth are falling out and growing in again. Dogs have more teeth than humans, averaging at around 42 total. As they come in, their gums will hurt, and you might find blood or drool on your puppy's bed, toys, or mouth (Donovan, 2015).

Chew toys are a must during this period, and I am sure you've figured that out already. In many cases, a good toy on its own isn't enough during the peak of the teething season. Here are a few things you can do to ease the process for you and your poor puppy.

- **Freeze the toys.** That's right, in your freezer! Many toys designed for chewing/teething can be put in the freezer safely. Giving your puppy a cold toy is a great way to pique their interest with something new while numbing their gums' pain in the process.

- Have **treats** on you at all times to redirect the puppy from biting. Put a treat in your hand and make a fist. Sit yourself down in front of your puppy and give them the time to smell your hand. They will start to lick, once they do that you start petting them with your other hand. This way you are telling them to explore and focus on something good instead of biting.

- **Tire the dog out** through obedience training. This will make their brain a lot calmer and phases out the need for biting and nipping.

- **Discourage biting.** Your puppy might want to develop a bad biting habit around this time due to their urge to chew. You should try and train them out of this early on, so it doesn't become a habit.

  - To train your puppy out of biting, give them a reaction every time. It can be a loud '*ouch!*' or another short, high-pitched sound. Puppies will understand this as a bad reaction, making it an effective correction tool (Donovan, 2015). You can also use a chew toy to discourage biting. When your puppy backs away or stops biting, reward them. If they keep biting, remove them from the situation quietly. It means putting them in their crate or leaving the room, so they get no more playtime. Make sure you make your reaction as boring as possible, so they do not feel rewarded for being worked up.

- Make sure you always have an eye on the use of your hands during this time. If you find your puppy is biting your hands during training, redirection, or playtime, you need to keep them out of reach. Making it impossible for them to bite your hands is a good way to break the habit. I know it sounds so simple and obvious but many people forget this step completely. What you can use instead are toys: balls on ropes for instance, a tug toy that you can hold on one end and your puppy on the other. If the dog nips your hand anyway, yell a loud 'ouch' and freeze. You need to go against your own instincts by not pulling your hand back. Keep your hand right there with your puppy and use your body language to tell them they've crossed the line. Don't push your hand towards the puppy either, just hold it right there. After that, always reinforce the behavior you do want.

My Puppy Hates When I Clip His Nails and Clean His Ears, How Can I Make This Easier?

Trimming your dog's nails and cleaning their ears is an important part of ownership. This responsibility is vital to making sure your puppy grows up to be healthy, comfortable, and strong. Your vet will be able to take care of many routine maintenance jobs your dog's body needs, but day-to-day hygiene concerns are more easily done at home. You don't want to have to take your puppy to the vet every time their nails grow a little too long.

Your handling training that we went over in Chapter 3 will come in handy here. If you've been keeping it up regularly, your puppy should be used to having their paws, ears, face, etc., touched, at least by you. Some puppies may have a slower time getting used to this, and that's okay, but you should keep exposing them to these parts of handling. It is the only way you will be able to get through clipping and cleaning sessions with no fuss.

Nail Clipping Tips

◆ Start with your puppy somewhere that is both comfortable and easy for you to restrain them. You should be able to pet them and grab their paws without having to get up. Your lap is an excellent place to start and should make them feel safe.

◆ You can also use a nail grinder instead of a clipper if you find it a more comfortable experience for you and your puppy.

◆ Introduce the clipper or grinder slowly to your puppy, as you do with other new objects. Let your puppy sniff and touch the grinder on their own at first, then reward them. Gently touch each paw with the clipper or grinder, and then give them another reward. Practice clipping around the puppy so they can hear the sound and see it move, and reward. Then, ease them into the actual trimming. Start with one nail at a time, then two, etc., with rewards between each milestone. This will make it seem less scary the first time you do a full trim.

◆ Knowing where to trim is essential. Some puppies have black nails, and some have white nails. With black nails, you cannot see what is called the "quick" of the nail. The quick is a bundle of blood vessels and nerves that you should never touch with a trimmer. If you clip too short and hit the quick, it can hurt your puppy and give them a bad association with clipping in the future.

◆ With white nails, you can see the quick easier. It looks like a dark, red, or pink line in the middle of the nail, kind of like a vein. For black nails, you can use the nail curve to figure out how far to trim. Always clip towards the tip of where the nail curves downward (Eldredge, 2017). When in doubt, don't clip too far, and stop early if you think you might be getting too close.

◆ When you go to the vet, you can have them clip your puppy's nails once in front of you, to show you the best way to judge how close you are to the quick.

- For puppies that hate clipping no matter what, reward them with treats throughout the process. They can get a treat when they are calm, and at the end of each successful clip, at first (Eldredge, 2017).

- If your puppy gets through one paw successfully, you can always take a break at that point and do the other paw tomorrow. Breaking it up into smaller sessions might make it less stressful for your puppy, and they will be more cooperative in the future.

Ear Cleaning Tips

- When your puppy is in a good mood, relaxed, or otherwise enjoying your company, put extra focus on handling their ears. Flip them up and look inside, and give them a good behind-the-ear scratch when you're done. It will make their ears less sensitive to the touches of being cleaned.

- During ear cleaning, have treats ready. After one ear, reward them with a treat, but only once the cleaning is done, and the puppy has calmed down. Then, move to the other ear, and repeat the same reward system.

How Do I Deal With Resource Guarding and a Possessive Puppy?

If my story about Rex reminds you of anything going on with your pup, you might be dealing with resource guarding. This can happen for a lot of different reasons. Sometimes it can be because a puppy came from a home where resources were scarce. In other cases, a puppy can pick up the habit simply because they like something a lot, and their instincts tell them to protect it.

This problem should be tackled one step at a time to get rid of the habit. The most important thing to remember when you start is that you should not use standard corrections for this behavior. This will validate your dog's concern that their item is in danger of being taken away.

Do not:

- Verbally reprimand the dog.

- Take the item away without replacing it.

- Lock them away from the item in a punishment zone where they can see the object.

- Use aggressive language or actions.

- Bribe your dog.

These behaviors will stress your dog out even more, which increases the amount they feel the need to guard. Instead, you can train your puppy to expect you and your hands around their stuff, and be more comfortable giving you control over it in the future.

With a food bowl:

1. Train your puppy to think that your hands are welcome around the food bowl because they bring more food. Start by putting down an empty bowl at the usual feeding time. When your puppy sniffs it, wait until they look to you, expecting food.

2. Add a handful of food to the bowl. Wait for the puppy to eat it, then add another.

3. Keep doing this until your puppy has eaten the usual amount of food. Over time, this will show them that there is nothing wrong with you standing near the food bowl, reaching towards it, or even touching the food (Simpawtico Training, n.d.).

With an item:

1. If you find them with the item already, let them keep it as long as it isn't something dangerous to them. Taking it away or forcing it out of their mouth will only teach them to be sneakier or more aggressive about their guarding.

2. Teach trading. Bring another object that is interesting to your puppy that they do not feel protective over. Let them look at it, smell it, etc. Then, remove the item, and give them a few treats. This will teach them that if they let you take an item away, they get a reward!

3. Keep practicing this with more and more interesting things. Use a valuable toy, piece of food, etc., to practice the trading exercise. You want to teach the puppy that giving something up is good and gets a reward. This is NOT a bribe, so do not show the puppy the treats until the object has been given up.

4. Try it with the actual item. After you've done the above practice exercise many times, approach your dog when they have the guarded object. If you can, set it up for them at a time when they don't already have the item. Put it out in front of them, try to take it back, and then provide the treat.

5. Repeat in phases until your puppy demonstrates more comfortability with you being around their favorite thing (Simpawtico Training, n.d.).

Finally, make sure you never reward your puppy when they are showing signs of resource guarding (Simpawtico Training, n.d.). If, at any time during these exercises, your puppy snarls, hunches, or bites at you, do not provide the expected reward. You don't want to reinforce behaving this way as a good thing.

My Puppy Is Digging Up the Whole Yard—How Do I Handle It?

Don't worry. Your puppy is not especially naughty for wanting to dig, no matter how annoying it may be. It's a part of their natural instincts, and some breeds dig more than others as a result. This doesn't make it any less of a problem for your beautiful yard, though, and it can pose risks like escaping under a fence or finding something hazardous in the dirt. There are a few ways you can prevent your dog from digging in a problematic way.

- Never leave the puppy alone in the yard for too long. Eventually, they'll get bored, and digging will become a habit.

- Put a variety of enrichment toys in the yard. It will keep them occupied with more productive things when they're outside and forget about digging.

- Redirect your dog's attention. When you catch them in the act, immediately pull the pup into a game, exercise, or trick. If they go along with it, reward the switch.

- Ensure your pup is getting enough exercise and stimulation in their daily training, playtime, and routine. Your puppy won't look for alternate ways to release that pent-up energy if they have spent it all already (Gibeault, 2019b).

Furry Finesse (weeks 13-14)

H ere as we enter the exciting second month of training, you can start working on making those basics like sit, stay, and down a little less basic. This means training your puppy to hold them longer, perform them in chaotic situations, and further away. Duration, distractions, and distance are the three tenants you can use to improve the core of your puppy's training knowledge. It will polish up those basic exercises and prep your dog to learn more exciting tricks along the way.

There was a dog in Nalu's training class that was great at all of the essential exercises. Her name was Daisy, and she could sit on command, stay without a treat, and raise her paw when asked. It was very impressive until the training class started to get a little more crowded.

The new problem was that as soon as another dog owner would say sit or get out a treat for their puppy, Daisy would lose focus and run over to them to get involved. She would try to sit, but for the wrong owner, and then she'd expect a treat! Other

'Dogs' lives are too short. Their only fault, really.'

- AGNES SLIGH TURNBULL

distractions were a problem too, like people coming and going through the door and chew toys that belonged to other puppies. Eventually, they had to take her back to square one on everything, because she had never learned to keep her attention on one thing at a time.

You should still be repeating exercises from previous weeks and incorporating them into your sessions. The things we'll learn this week can be used to work on the duration, distraction, and distance of those exercises, so you should apply them to your repetitions whenever possible.

Weekly Goals

This week is all about toughening the power of the commands your puppy

already understands and expanding upon them.

Week Six Goal: Strengthen the basics and move on to more complicated tricks.

You will be surprised how much your bond between you and your puppy has grown since you first met. Your puppy knows how training works at this stage, and you can use that knowledge to build more confidence.

Frequently Asked Questions

Your pup is capable of more than you might expect, and they will look to you for approval every time they learn something new. This next section will show you how to use the strong bond developed between you and your puppy to go above and beyond in training.

How Do I Improve the Duration, Distractions, and Distance of Our Training Exercises?

You should already be practicing your basic commands during almost every training session. When you do so, use these steps to lengthen the amount of time, focus, and distance your puppy can handle. It will make the commands more effective outside of training sessions, and you can use them in any given situation.

Here are some examples for duration, distractions, and distance, with different tricks, as designed by the International Association of Animal Behavior Consultants (Tyler, 2010). You can apply the same principles from one trick to another to train on a specific skill.

Duration - Sit

1. Start your usual sit training with the same amount of treats as always. While they're sitting, provide a few treats in a row, up until your puppy can't stay still anymore.

2. Start slowing down the rewards one repetition at a time. After your puppy sits, give one treat, wait three seconds, then another, wait three seconds, then another.

3. Repeat this, extending the time between treats from three seconds to six. Next time, extend to nine and continue this way with a longer period each time.

4. Do this every time you train on 'sit,' making your puppy expect these longer waiting periods between treats.

5. Add 'sit' to other parts of the day where there is a natural reward. Make your puppy sit before going outside, coming back in, putting on a leash, getting their toy back after tug of war, etc. Introducing rewards in day-to-day life will help your puppy understand that 'sit' doesn't end until you say it ends (Tyler, 2010).

Distractions - Lie Down

1. Add intentional distractions to the environment. Some examples could be toys, treats, tissue paper, or other exciting objects.

2. Observe how your dog interacts with these distractions. Take note of the warning signs your dog might exhibit when something is distracting them.

3. During your training on 'down,' go back to basics. Be ready to provide more rewards and expect your dog to give into the new distractions around them.

4. When your puppy starts to get up too early, or look away from you during training, lure their attention back to you with a treat. Reward them after they maintain that focus for a few seconds.

5. Repeat until your puppy has eyes on you and only you. End the session on this successful note.

6. Continue doing this with different distractions in different areas of the house. Practice expecting your puppy to lie down and watch you, even when outside or in other highly distracting places.

7. When your puppy is doing well, add steps from duration training, to lengthen the amount of time you expect your puppy to remain focused before getting a reward (Tyler, 2010).

Distance - Stay

1. Start in a calm environment with minimal distractions. Adding distance to an exercise is going to be a bigger change than you might expect.

2. Move one step at a time. Get your dog to sit, and then stay, as usual. Provide a reward after a few seconds.

3. Take one step backward. Say 'stay' again, and then return to the dog and provide a treat. Repeat a few times, with just one step.

4. Take two steps this time. Say 'stay' again, then return to the dog and provide a treat. Repeat a few times.

5. Keep doing this, extending the distance by one step every time, and rewarding your dog after a few moments of staying. You should also try stepping left and right, circling your dog in different directions (Tyler, 2010).

6. Practice this over and over before you extend the duration of long-distance stays. The longer the distance, the shorter the duration, until your puppy gets the hang of it.

7. At the end of this exercise, reward your puppy and give them the release word.

8. If at any time your puppy gets up and runs at you when they should be staying, say 'no' and gently put them back in their original spot. Start the exercise from scratch.

What Are Some More Advanced Exercises We Can Learn?

Some people love to teach their pooch very cool tricks. And you know what, why not make your puppy a good candidate to join the circus, huh?! If your little furry friend is into this kind of stuff, you should definitely give it a go. Let's see a couple of options you have:

Spin

1. Start with your puppy on their feet and a few treats in hand.

2. Lure your puppy with the treat. It should be pretty easy to lure them in a slow circle or a spin. Stay in one direction every time, for now.

3. After your puppy completes the circle, mark and reward with a treat. It might take a bit for the puppy to catch onto the circle pattern, but keep trying and reward only after the circle is complete.

4. Once your puppy gets good at spinning, remove the treats from your luring hand. Use the same hand gesture to lure the puppy into a spin. Once complete, mark and reward with goodies from the non-luring hand.

5. Keep practicing this until your puppy is able to spin on the hand gesture alone, then add a verbal command. You can use 'spin' or 'twirl' or anything you like, as long as it is consistent.

6. Start with the command this time, then make the hand gesture as always. Mark and reward after a full circle.

7. Repeat like this until you feel comfortable using the command alone. Continue rewarding at the end of the spin, but gradually wean the pup off the hand gesture (Greenwald, 2019).

Roll Over

1. Start with practicing 'lie down' a few times. Then, while the puppy is still lying down, begin the roll-over exercise.

2. With a few treats in hand, lure your dog into lying down if they aren't already. Give the treat up close, right near the puppy's nose.

3. Next, bring another treat to the puppy's nose, and slowly lure them by the nose to look up and start to roll onto their back. It might take a few tries.

4. Give them the treat once the puppy is on their back or close to it. With another treat in hand, lure them further over to continue the roll.

5. Once your puppy is on its other side, give another treat.

6. Bring the next treat out and a few inches away from your puppy's nose, so they have to complete the roll to see it. Give them the treat and plenty of praise for completing the first roll.

7. Repeat these steps over and over until your puppy gets the hang of the rolling action. It might take a while, but it should get better each time.

8. After a few repetitions, pair a 'roll over' command and hand gesture at the beginning. The motion can be spinning your finger in a circle or something similar that mimics your luring hand pattern.

9. Continue practicing this regularly, and as your puppy gets better at it, reduce the treats. Eventually, you should only provide a treat after the full roll is completed (Simpawtico, 2016).

Play Dead

1. Start learning this trick after your puppy has gotten good at rolling over.

2. Practice the first steps of 'roll over,' but use the command 'play dead' instead.

3. Halfway through luring your puppy over, interrupt it by giving the puppy a big belly rub with lots of praise and good scratches.

4. Pair the belly rub with something like 'good play dead' or 'good job,' so they know this is a reward.

5. Repeat, using the belly rub as the main reward, but supplementing with treats afterward if needed (Simpawtico, 2016).

Shake

1. Start with a few treats in your hand, in a closed fist. Hold the fist out to the puppy and let them sniff it.

2. The pup will try to get the treat, but don't open your fist. Wait until your puppy naturally raises its paw to your hand to try and get at the treat.

3. When your puppy's paw touches your hand, mark the behavior, then open your hand and let them have the treat.

4. Repeat this a few times, then switch to an empty fist with no treat. Wait until your puppy paws at the hand again, mark, and reward with a treat from your other hand.

5. Once your puppy gets the hang of this, add a verbal cue. Right before you hold out your hand, say 'shake' or 'paw.' Then do everything from Step 4. Repeat a few times.

6. Start replacing your closed fist with an open hand and lengthening the amount of time your puppy's paw needs to stay in the hand before they get a treat.

7. If your puppy removes their hand too early, repeat 'shake' and wait for their paw to come back to give them a treat.

8. Eventually, you can replace the treat with praise, for when you want to show off this adorable trick more often (Greenwald, 2019).

9. If your puppy is not getting the hang of this trick right away, you can gently guide their paw to you by grabbing their leg and bringing it up. It will show them what they are expected to do.

What Games Can I Play With My Puppy?

Training exercises are not the only important part of puppy life. Believe it or not, play is just as important, if not more so. Most puppies love some alone time with their toys, but you should also play some games with them one on one. I've included some of my favorite games that are fun for people and pups alike. We're are only talking about these games in week six in this book, but actually, you should start with these exercises as soon as you can. Puppies need distraction from all of their training, just like children need playtime in-between classes in school.

Find It

This game is a great way to have fun with your puppy, get them used to all sorts of places in the house, and learn a new command. You can do this exercise on a leash at first if you feel it is necessary (Ultimate Puppy, 2015).

1. While you set up, have your puppy be in another room, in the crate, or otherwise not observing you.

2. Hide pieces of kibble or tiny treats all around the house. At first, these can be easy to find, and you can up the challenge later.

3. Bring your puppy out, and introduce the phrase 'find it!' in an executed voice. Repeat it as your puppy starts to smell the food nearby.

4. If your puppy starts finding the treats on their own, let them, while repeating the command more excitedly, the closer they get to each treat.

5. If your puppy needs help or encouragement, use your finger to tap the ground near the treat and say 'find it!' again. Keep doing this for each treat.

6. Each time the pup finds a treat, reward them more with praise and pets. You can mark the behavior with 'good job,' or 'you got it,' or something like that.

7. Once you've played a few times, make the treats harder to find, but keep using 'find it.' You can gradually teach your puppy to understand that this command means it's time to search for something, whether it is for the game or to find something new in their domain (Ultimate Puppy, 2015).

Pick a Hand

This game is easy to understand for most puppies and can be played easily with other family members or friends that aren't used to training with the pup. It also puts the puppy's 'shake' skills to practice.

1. When your puppy isn't looking, put a treat or some kibble in one hand, and nothing in the other.

2. Put both hands out to your puppy, and say 'find it' or 'shake' if you want to reinforce that trick.

3. When your puppy puts the paw on a hand or touches the hand with their nose, open it. If it's the right hand, they get the treat. If it's wrong, show the puppy which hand the treat was in, but do not give it to them.

4. Start the game over if your puppy got it wrong, and always end the game after a round where they got it right. It will teach your puppy to be a critical thinker and communicate more effectively with you (Ultimate Puppy, 2015).

Follow the Leader

This game is great as you get into week seven of training, where we will be focusing on longer walks and leash training. Playing with your puppy will make it clear that following you is fun and gets rewards outside of regular training and walks. This game should always be done in the yard because you'll need a lot of space (Ultimate Puppy, 2015).

1. Find a toy or treat that your puppy loves, and get it ready. Let them know you have it, and then run from them!

2. If your puppy doesn't immediately follow you, come back around and tease them with the toy, drop some treats behind you. Make sure you are making exciting noises and showing them how much fun you're having.

3. Once they're following, change your path. Go fast and slow, left and right, etc.

4. Stop for a few seconds and practice a command your pup is good at. Sit, stay, lie down, etc. Make them hold it, give a treat.

5. Start the chase again.

6. Stop for a few seconds and reward your pup with playtime! Play a quick game of "pick a hand" or get rowdy with a toy.

7. Start the chase again.

8. Repeat this, rewarding the pup for following you, and taking breaks here and there where they must pay attention to you for something important or fun.

9. This game is not a substitute for leash or recall training, but it will reinforce your puppy's behavior with you while you move around. They should be used to following you and paying attention to what you want them to do. This game helps with that, and it burns a lot of energy (Ultimate Puppy, 2015).

These are just a couple of ideas to get your started. Get creative though, just like your puppy! You can do some fun (brain) games with your pup using everyday life items that you would normally throw away. And most of all, have fun !!

A Walk in the Park... Or Not! (weeks 14-15)

By 14-15 weeks, hopefully, your puppy has had all of its shots. Check with your vet, and if your puppy is vaccinated, you can start focusing on leash training and walks. Because of this, chapter seven is all about leashes, walking etiquette, and frequently asked questions about the world of walking puppies. You might be thrilled to get your pup out and about at last or worried about the daunting responsibility of taking them into the real world. Don't be too nervous. Every puppy can learn to walk, and yes, even be calm while on the leash.

Take my neighbor Marsha's Golden Doodle Bucky, for example. Bucky loved the idea of walks from the very beginning and still gets excited every time they go out together. The problem is that Bucky did not love the leash from the beginning. He would run from it and even try to hide it if he got it off the hook when his mom wasn't looking. Eventually, he learned that there would be no walk without the leash, so he tried to get smart about it.

He would allow the leash and behave well enough until they were a few minutes into the walk. Once

'Whoever said you can't buy happiness forgot little puppies.'

- GENE HILL

they got out into the open sidewalk, wind in his fur, he would start biting at the leash and trying his best to wriggle out of it. What was she going to do, put him in the crate? The crate was nowhere to be seen! I presume that this was going through his head when I saw him running down the street towards my house, Marsha frantically trying to catch up with him.

He didn't get far, of course, but eventually, Bucky and Marsha had to go back to day one on leash training. No matter how well he behaved at the beginning of the walk, he would always try and pull a fast one on her half-way through.

If you don't want to deal with your own runaway Bucky situation, there are some precautions you can take during the early days of leash training.

Weekly Goals

Walking is what this week is all about. You have already introduced the leash itself to your puppy, whether they liked it or not. Now it's time to show them what it's for.

Week Seven Goal: Be prepared for the highs and lows of walking your puppy.

For most dogs, there's more to it than just hooking it on and walking around, so we'll cover some of the most common problems so you can prepare for them ahead of time. If you feel that you need to focus on basics more before taking them out into the world, that's okay. You do not need to start walk training until you are both ready.

Frequently Asked Questions

Good preparation will involve easing your puppy into the length of the walk, redirecting behavior like biting and chewing on the leash, and slowly loosening the leash. Over time, you and your puppy will build mutual trust.

If you can trust your puppy to behave, your puppy can trust you to lead the walk without restricting them too much.

How Long Can I Walk My Puppy?

Every puppy is a little different, so it depends. A dog's breed, attitude, and general fitness will come into play (Burke, 2017). A large dog like a Great Dane might be able to take a much longer walk than a little Pomeranian. Their walking speed might also impact how long you are out of the house, versus how long of a distance you actually walk. Research information about your dog's breed to start with.

Either way, you should start off shorter than you expect. Puppies can go from balls of energy to balls of sleep at the drop of a hat. If you plan too long of a walk, you might find yourself carrying a puppy home for half the journey.

According to the U.K. Kennel Club, puppies should get at least five minutes of exercise per month of age (Animal Planet, 2013). That means a three-month-old puppy should get at least fifteen minutes of exercise, and a four-month puppy should get at least twenty. At fifteen weeks old, your puppy is right in the middle of that range. Not all of that exercise will come in the form of walking, so you can start with a 5-10 minute long walk and see how your puppy handles it. Remember, this is a guideline, not a strict rule. Every pup is different, and yours might need more or less than this. Use it as a starting point, but pay attention to your puppy's needs.

How Do I Keep My Puppy From Biting the Leash?

When your puppy bites the leash, you never want to reward that behavior. They might be doing it because they are irritated with the leash or just because they want to play. Make sure you are paying attention to your dog's behavior before, throughout, and after the walk. If your dog needs more attention or stimulation, you can fix these problems before the leash goes on. Here are a few ways to try and handle it, depending on your puppy's needs (Farricelli, 2021).

- Play or exercise before the walk. If your puppy is full of energy before going on the walk, they might not be getting enough activity with walking alone. You don't want to walk an exhausted puppy, but you could try to introduce an active play or training session before the walk.

- Redirect with the use of treats. You can do this with the 'find it' game introduced in the last chapter, as one example. When your dog is going for the leash, throw a few treats around on the ground, and say 'find it!' in an excited voice. Interrupting the biting behavior with something fun or positive will keep it from becoming a habit (Farricelli, 2021).

- Bring a special toy. This toy should be something they can bite and chew and used exclusively for walks. When your puppy starts to bite the leash, get out the toy, wait for them to release the leash, walk towards you, and then play tug of war for a few moments. It acts as a reward for letting go and an outlet for that energy (Farricelli, 2021).

- Replace it. When your dog tries to bite the leash, replace that behavior with a command they are good at, like 'sit.' If your puppy is used to getting a reward for sitting, they will stop the leash-biting right away and sit to get that treat. You can eventually phase out the treat and use 'sit' as a way of telling your pup to back off the leash.

121

- Be smart with your leash. If you are having a rough time getting your puppy to stop chewing, change what you're using. Attaching a light piece of plastic or metal to the chain is less tempting to chew than that soft leash fabric. When they try to bite it, they'll find it isn't as satisfying and stop trying (Farricelli, 2021).

- You can also use a high-value treat to lure the puppy away from the leash. Get it out and wait until they let go of the leash. Make them sit or walk a few steps back, prompting the dog to follow you. Then, give them the treat.

How Can I Teach My Puppy to Walk on a Loose Leash?

Going from a tighter leash (never too tight) to a loose leash is an important graduation process during the early stages of leash training. At first, you will not want your puppy to stray very far from you, but it is easier in the long run if they can move around on their own terms. Only after they have earned your trust should loose leashes be acceptable. Follow these tips to make that easier.

Heel Exercise

Heeling is essential for loose leash walking. A loose leash does not mean that your puppy gets to run free, just that there is no tension on the leash. You can use the heel exercise to have them follow you without tugging on the leash. If you haven't taken the time to train 'heel', then go back to chapter 1, question 3. Here's a short recap:

1. Walk forward a few steps, then turn around and say 'heel.'

2. Say 'good heel,' and provide a reward.

3. Repeat Steps 1 and 2 until your puppy starts to follow as soon as you say 'heel,' with no tug on the leash. Eventually, your puppy will understand that 'heel' means to follow, but it may take some practice.

The Actual Walk

1. Train before the walk. You should practice a few commands before going on long walks with a loose leash. Commands like 'heel,' 'good,' 'come', 'break' and 'leave it' are great tools while you are out and about.

2. Go back to your recall exercise and ask your dog to come back to you. You can use the phrase 'come' or 'come here'.

3. Practice these cues on a short walk and take plenty of treats with you.

4. If your puppy does well with these short walks, lengthen them with a looser leash. Use the known commands when your puppy strays too far, and if they follow them, give them a treat.

5. If your puppy pulls on the leash, refuses to come when called, or wanders off without your lead, you need to go back to your basic obedience exercises. This just simply means that your foundation work isn't strong enough and your pup needs more practice.

Throughout the walk, reward your puppy for paying attention to you. If they look up at you, mark and reward. If they start to get distracted by something, grab their attention first, and reward that redirection with a treat. When you stop, get out a treat and have them 'sit,' then reward them when they stop with you (Donovan, 2019).

How Do I Stop My Puppy From Pulling the Leash in Front of Me?

Start by never, ever rewarding a pull on the leash. If your puppy tries to pull you somewhere, do not give in. You should also never yank your puppy back. Pulling them will only make them want to play tug of war or feel antagonized. Instead, you should shut down the fun immediately. Keep a firm grasp on the leash, and stop in your spot. Be a statue, do not budge, and do not acknowledge your puppy until they return to you. Once you have their attention, start the walk again like nothing happened (Donovan, 2019).

If you are having this issue, you should go back to the 'heel' command we've looked in chapter 1. This is a great way to deal with pulling and keeping your dog by your side.

Can I Go to the Dog Park Now?

The short answer is yes, but I don't think it is the best idea just yet. If your dog behaves well on the leash, and you know the people at the park, it might be okay. An easy-going puppy paired with dogs that you know are well-trained does not pose much of a risk, but if the other dogs are rowdy, uncontrolled, or unsocialized, this could ruin your puppy's first experience with the park. The decision is yours. Just make sure you are confident in your puppy's abilities and that you know how to leave the park quickly if there is a bad situation about to happen. There is nothing wrong with waiting or not going to the park at all.

What Should I Avoid While Walking My Puppy?

Here are some of the most common mistakes you can make while dog-walking. Some of these may seem harmless, or even tempting, but they can cause bad associations and danger for your pup:

- Roller-skating and bicycle rides. Your puppy can't handle this yet because their bones are still growing and it might ruin their growth

- Long walks. The rule of thumb, like I mentioned before, in many books is usually 5 minutes of exercise per month of age. If you have a highly active dog though, this might not be enough. Adapt the 5-minute rule to whatever your puppy can handle. But keep in mind to not overdo it. You can always add obedience training and brain games to the mix to tire your puppy out.

- Face-to-face meetups with other dogs when walking on leash. This can potentially cause friction between both dogs. The leash always provides a certain amount of tension and a feeling of 'not being able to get away'. Some dogs will find this leash meetup very scary and don't know how to handle it. As a result they might become either frightened or aggressive. You want to avoid these types of situations at all times, even when the other person says their dog is one of the good ones.

♦ Yanking the leash at the wrong moment. A little tug on the leash tells your dog there are boundaries they cannot cross and they need to follow your lead. Anxiety or aggression can be two counter reactions from your dog towards you in this situation. If you need to pop the leash for some reason, keep in mind that you only have 1 second to do that before your dog doesn't even know anymore why you did it.

♦ Using the 'come' word for anything less than an amazing reward. Puppies especially are usually very food or toy motivated. Use that to your advantage! Think about how you train your dog because anything you ask them to do, you need to be sure they can achieve. If not, you'll find yourself repeating every command multiple times. Something you actually want to avoid at all cost.

How Do I Introduce Public Transportation?

For those who take a bus or a train around the city, it can be nice to take your dog with you. A well-trained dog can have fulfilling rides on public transport by your side, and that can make it easier for you to take longer walks or bring them to the park/vet/etc., without being stuck in the car. Your puppy should be leash trained before you try this, so feel free to come back to this question later if they aren't ready yet.

♦ Start with walks to the station and back. The people, sounds, and business of the place might scare your puppy and reveal a behavior you didn't expect. Some dogs forget their training when put into a situation with more humans than usual, and this first step is important to socialize your puppy with crowds of strangers properly.

At first, you might only go to the station's entrance and go further in over time (Dogs for Good, 2016). Go as far as your puppy seems calm and happy, and head home at the first sign of stress.

◆ Once your puppy is comfortable going to the station and/or being at the bus stop, sit on a bench there for a period. This is a good moment to provide a treat or a chew toy. Sit there for as long as you are both comfortable, and then walk home again. It will get your puppy used to the pacing of a transport trip.

◆ Take your first ride on a short route, one stop or two both ways, etc. Ensure that you don't push it too far, or you will have a hard time getting home.

◆ Bring treats and interesting toys (filled Kong, chew toy) for the journeys as you extend them (Dogs for Good, 2016). Giving your puppy something to focus on will make the experience less stressful and keep them from being too rude to other humans if they are excited.

◆ You can practice some of your tricks like sit, paw, lie down, etc., on the bus if your pup is calm enough. It is an excellent way to teach them to be focused during the ride.

Ruff Ruff Recap Continued (weeks 15-16 = 2 Month Goal)

F ind your puppy and give them a big belly rub because you're finally here! It has been two exciting and exhausting months of training, and you are in the last stage of training this guide has to offer you. At this stage, you have loaded so much information into your brain and your puppy's brain that it might seem like you haven't mastered any of it. That's okay! These first two months are the best time for you to introduce all of the basics and build upon them, but no one expects you to have perfected them. Even if you are still struggling with potty training, sitting, or crate training, your pup will get the hang of it eventually.

This is why it is most essential for you to spend this final week recapping everything you've learned so far, and making sure you have solidified a rock-hard training schedule.

"You don't always get the dog you want, but you get the dog that you need.'

- CESAR MILLAN

Weekly Goals

For this week, your goal is simple. Go through the checklist from Chapter 4, and then go through this checklist too. By the end, you should know where you stand on every single training topic. Then, develop a new schedule to reinforce the most important exercises for you and your pup.

Week Eight Goal: Evaluate the strengths and weaknesses of your puppy training so far.

Once you know what still needs work, you can focus on those things as you face the weeks to come. What's important is that you do not drop anything completely. As always, even the most simple exercises will need repetition to keep them fresh.

Recap

After the first month, you did this with everything from weeks one through four. Now it's time to do it again, with weeks one through four and five through eight combined. It's time to make sure you haven't been neglecting any part of your training and discover where your puppy still needs work for the future.

Teething

By now, you should have a good idea of how much teething will be a problem. In many cases, puppies have forgotten the habit by two months or switched to chewing toys. It is still common for some puppies to be struggling at this stage, though, as they are still growing in new teeth. Don't forget to interrupt your puppy only when you see them chewing and not when you find the aftermath. Using frozen toys, washcloths, and other cold and safe chewables will help relieve the pain in your puppies mouth. Teach them to come to you for the right chew toys when they need them.

Handling Practice

Clipping nails and cleaning ears is never fun, but it is necessary. Make sure you are doing it on a regular basis and that you establish a routine at this early stage. The more you get through the trouble spots now, the easier it will be when they're older or dealing with more invasive procedures at the vet. When you aren't clipping or cleaning, pet your puppy's paws and ears, and get them used to trusting human touch as much as possible. It never hurts to ask your vet to show you how to do something if you have trouble at home, too.

Digging

How many holes are in your yard so far? Whether that answer is zero or 100, you should still be supervising your puppy in the yard. Leaving them unattended for too long will make them bored, and a bored puppy is bound to figure out how digging works eventually. Anxiety, excess energy, and under-stimulation are other common reasons your puppy might be digging. Make sure you evaluate how your puppy feels before you come up with the best solution.

Duration, Distraction, and Distance

If your puppy is a master at anything by this point, great news! It's time for you to make that exercise a little harder. Lengthening the duration your puppy has to sit, stay, or shake is a great way of teaching discipline and patience. Adding distractions to your training environment will make it easier for your puppy to ignore them when out on a walk or in an emergency situation. Teaching your puppy to follow your commands no matter how far away you are will make it much easier for you to train on the go and call for your puppy when you have something for them.

Advanced Tricks

Rolling over, playing dead, spinning in circles, and shaking are all great tricks to bring out for friends and guests when you want to show off your smart pup. They're also great for growing that puppy brain and strengthening your relationship. If you think a particular trick is useful or just cute, go ahead and try to teach it to your puppy. They are capable of learning anything, as long as you take it one step at a time.

Walking

The most important thing to remember when walking your puppy is that this is a slower process than you might imagine. Some puppies adapt to long walks pretty quickly, but that doesn't mean they will behave well on every walk. Make sure you aren't pushing your puppy too far too fast, and be ready for new behaviors to crop up outside the house.

CHAPTER NINE

Exciting Extras

Not everything needs to be taught in a specific week, or one week at a time. Here are a few important things to introduce to your puppy and keep in mind as you continue your adventure together.

Swimming

You might not think it's useful to teach your puppy to swim, but when you need it, it comes in handy. I went through a scary situation with Reece a few years ago, which taught me the value of teaching dogs to swim early on. When we were on a walk, Reece saw a bird, and because we were still working on distraction training, he shot off after it. Reece is a big dog, and I lost control of him at that moment. He sprinted after the bird, over a hill, and fell into a stream that neither of us could see. We both got scared because we hadn't known there was anything unsafe there. Fortunately, Reece knew how to swim, and he was able to get to shore to shake everywhere and get us both wet.

Once you have mastered some of the basics with your puppy and have good control over them, you

'A lot of shelter dogs are mutts like me."

- BARACK OBAMA

can look into swim training. It is usually done in a controlled environment with a puppy life-jacket at first. Swimming can be a fun activity for you both and a great outlet for burning that extra energy.

Loud Noises

Thunderstorms are the most common source of this issue with puppies. Many dogs are afraid of thunder, garbage trucks, vacuums, and other loud noises. In some cases, this can lead to a long-term anxiety problem for your puppy. The best way to approach a puppy with a fear of loud noises might not be what you think. Your instinct may be to hug and pet your puppy during a storm and give them treats to cheer up. **Do not do this.** It will reward your puppy for cowering, barking, or hiding from the sound, and they will think you agree with how scary it is. Petting a dog during a fearful moment is like saying, 'You're right, we should be scared. Great instincts!'

Instead of hugging your dog in these moments, just give them assistance by staying close. No petting, no talking to your dog, just being near so the puppy feels supported and not alone. Another thing you can do is tell them what behavior you want to see from them. This makes you the leader in a tense situation and will help your dog immensely. You can tell them to go to their bed, or another safe place, and stay there.

If this does not change their behavior, you can try to condition them to associate the noises with good things during the day. See the section on vacuuming if you want some more ideas on fixing your puppy's association with loud noises.

Vet Visits

Not everyone knows how often to take a puppy to the vet at first. The truth is, you should take the puppy in as much as possible, even if they aren't due for any shots and are feeling healthy. Taking your puppy to the vet frequently in the first few months will desensitize them to the experience and make it less scary as an adult. Many adult dogs who are afraid of the vet just haven't been exposed to it enough as a puppy.

Try to take your puppy for a short visit as often as possible, depending on how calm they are during the experience. If your vet is okay with it, you can take them in just to walk around the lobby, get some pets from the front counter, and see their vet's face. It will strengthen the relationship between the puppy and the vet, making it a friendly place and not a place of nightmares.

More than one dog in the house

Start training your dogs one at a time. This is crucial to have success in the long run. If you train all of your dogs together, I can guarantee from my own experience, it's not going to go well. Don't worry if you have four dogs, you don't need to train them all for 30 to 45 minutes. What's important is to follow a schedule where each dog gets their alone time with you at the same time each day. A 15 minute training session is more than enough, as long as you repeat this at least twice a day. Or multiple times if you're up for it. But keep the schedule consistent.

Once again, consistency is key. Always take the same dog out first before the other. Dogs love structure and give you the best results when the pattern stays the same.

If the dogs love to play with each other, that could be the reward after your training sessions.

Keep in mind, this only applies to training. Walking on the other hand can be done with all of the dogs together.

But most of all, enjoy your time with each dog separately and be proud of your accomplishments, no matter how small they are. It's not an easy task to control multiple dogs. But with consistent training, you can get the most amazing results.

Conclusion

N ow that you've made it through two months of training, I have great news for you. You have many, many more months to go! Trust me, that IS good news. Training never truly ends, but it will get easier and more interesting the more you do it. For the next year, your puppy will still fall back into the same problems they had when you first brought them home. Your job is to catch them before they become habits and give your puppy the confidence and understanding they need to behave correctly.

There is no one way to train every puppy. Each dog is different, and each trainer is even more different. The needs of your puppy will vary wildly depending on breed, personality, intelligence, and your personal style of training. The experience you've gained over the past two months is invaluable to shaping what the rest of your journey looks like.

Do not be afraid to use tools and reminders. Take your list of house rules and put them somewhere. Your puppy might not be able to read them, but you can. Having the rules written down will make them feel more permanent and remind you that you

'A dog is the only thing on earth that loves you more than he loves himself.'

- JOSH BILLINGS

should never cave on what is important in your house. Your puppy will adapt. You do not need to let them rule the house just because they are a little feisty.

Go ahead and write down some checklists, too. Having a routine for your training session is the best way to make sure that your puppy learns the most efficiently. Puppies work best with patterns and repetition. It's just how their brain works. You might have to do the same exercise 1000 times before they even get it half right. No matter what, you need to bring consistency to every single training session. Having a daily or weekly schedule set in stone will help you hold yourself to the same high standards that you are setting for your puppy.

Potty training, crate training, and boundaries are fundamental building blocks to making the house a more comfortable place for your puppy. If your puppy knows the difference between what belongs to them and what belongs to you, they will not be confused when you have to reinforce the rules later on in training. When you encounter problems in these areas, try to figure out what is confusing your puppy. Is the bathroom always available? Is the crate the right size? Do you let your puppy wander around the house too much?

As you move on to verbal commands, tricks, outings, and adapting to the world, you will run into countless questions. Don't be afraid to refer back to this guide or to reach out to other dog owners. Anecdotes and advice are the best tools you have because you can always learn a new perspective from another trainer's creativity. Try to experiment with what works in your house and apply it to new training.

Use the concepts you've learned in early exercises and apply them to ones in the future, too. Redirection, desensitization, socialization, counter-conditioning, and other core components apply to every single activity you train on. You might not need them every time, but you should keep them in mind for when you run into a brick wall with a specific problem.

When in doubt, return to the basics. It could mean starting the exercise over again or returning to 'sit' if your puppy is having a hard time. Remember, your puppy cannot tell you verbally when they are overwhelmed or when you have gone past something too quickly that they don't understand quite yet. It is never a bad thing to practice something too much, but too little can be detrimental.

Finally, as you move on to the rest of your puppy adventure, remember to use positive reinforcement, correction, patience, consistency, and repetition. These are the most essential building blocks of good dog training, and they will still be relevant even when your puppy is 2, 5, or 10 years old.

Above all else, have fun! Training should always be fun, no matter how frustrating certain parts might become. If you are having any sort of problem in training, take a moment to step back and examine how you are teaching your puppy. Are they enjoying themselves? If not, they are not listening to you, and they will not learn anything. I promise that spending an exciting two hours going over the same two tricks will be much better with a happy puppy than a bored one.

Epilogue: Pepper's Story Revisited

Let's look back at the story we went over at the beginning of this guide. James and Pepper did not start off on the right paw together, and they both had a bad experience. James could not figure out why his puppy was not learning the right things and ended up giving up on the poor girl. We last left Pepper sitting in the car, feeling confused about what she did wrong and why she was being abandoned.

Luckily, this story has a happy ending, even if it didn't start perfectly. When Pepper was returned to the shelter, it didn't take long for her to find a new home. She was a young, cute puppy, so she was gladly adopted by Danielle, an aspiring puppy trainer.

Danielle had an easier time with Pepper's problems right away. She was no professional, for sure, but she was more prepared for the things she might run into with a new puppy. Even though Pepper was behind on a lot of the basics, Danielle set aside long training sessions to go through each exercise one step at a time and make sure that nothing went over the puppy's head. When Pepper ran into all of the same issues she did with James, they were handled a little better this time around.

First of all, potty training was still a struggle. Pepper had never figured out exactly where to go at home, and she was afraid of doing it wrong again at her new house. Danielle expected this, and brought Pepper to the right spot right away on the very first day, showing her where to go. She got it right at first, but she had a few accidents inside since she was nervous. It was because Pepper still didn't understand how to ask to go outside when she had to go pee, and she would get so anxious about it that she would hold it all day instead.

After a while, Danielle noticed this problem, and instead of punishing Pepper for making the mistake, she decided to come up with a better solution. Every half an hour, Danielle would take Pepper outside to the pee spot. At first, this was confusing too, because Pepper didn't always need to go. Then she figured out that when she DID go, she would get treats!! It was very exciting, and it made it clear to Pepper that she would get a reward when she peed in the right spot. When it was the wrong spot, there would be no reward. She found this very logical.

Pepper still liked treats a lot. She would bark and bark at Danielle for more treats, as she did with James, but this was weird too. Instead of giving her treats when she barked, Danielle totally ignored her. For whatever reason, barking didn't work on this new human. Over time, she learned that being quiet got her more treats than barking, and a lot of other things got her treats too. Sitting, staying, and following Danielle always got treats, or even better, pets! She learned to like pets more than treats, sometimes.

It took a little bit of time to adjust, but sooner or later, things all started to fall into place for Pepper and Danielle. Even when something took a few tries, Danielle never gave up, and Pepper never broke the rules if she understood them. It turned out that all the problems James had were actually because he didn't understand her puppy brain and didn't speak the same language. Now that Pepper knew the rules, and knew right and wrong, she never wanted to misbehave.

All of the things James tried to teach in the first month of training came later, on Pepper's terms. Taking things a little slower made it easier for her to learn advanced tricks like shaking and standing on her hind legs. Danielle even promised to take her to the dog park in a month if she was good!

Pepper never thought she would make it this far, but now she knows that she's able to be a good girl, as long as she has a friend that will show her how and believe in her.

FACEBOOK GROUP

Welcome to the Tribe!

If you want to get even more informative insights you can always join my Facebook group:

New Puppy & Dog Owners Tribe

(https://www.facebook.com/groups/dogownerstribe)

Scan the QR-code to easily join the Facebook Group

WE'VE GOT YOUR
QUESTIONS
COVERED

NEW PUPPY & DOG OWNERS TRIBE

LEAVE A REVIEW

Photo: Bill Stephan – Unsplash.com

I hope you found lots of good advice and tips on how to guide your little pup into becoming that well behaving companion for life!

For an independent author, book reviews are essential to continue publishing real value to the dog-loving public out there.

If you enjoyed the book I would be very grateful if you could take the time to leave an honest book review on the Amazon website.

Type the link below into your browser and it will take you straight to the review page:

amazon.com/review/create-review?&asin=B0942G6CJC

Thank you!

References

Animal Planet. (2013, January 11). *How much exercise does my puppy need?* Animal Planet. http://www.animalplanet.com/pets/how-much-exercise-does-a-puppy-need/

Arford, K. (2019, November 19). *Crate Training Benefits: Why A Crate Is Great For You And Your Dog.* American Kennel Club. https://www.akc.org/expert-advice/training/why-crate-training-is-great-for-your-dog/

Bender, A. (2019, November 4). *How to Teach a Dog to Play.* The Spruce Pets. https://www.thesprucepets.com/train-a-dog-to-play-1117214

Best Friends. (2019). *Building Confidence in Dogs.* Best Friends Animal Society. https://resources.bestfriends.org/article/building-confidence-dogs

Burke, A. (2017, November 8). *How Much Exercise Is Too Much for a Puppy?* American Kennel Club. https://www.akc.org/expert-advice/health/puppies-how-much-exercise/

Dogs for Good. (2016, November 8). *Introducing dogs to public transport.* Dogs for Good. https://www.dogsforgood.org/2016/11/introducing-dogs-to-public-transport/

Donovan, L. (2015, October 12). *Puppy Teething and Nipping: A Survival Guide.* American Kennel Club; American Kennel Club. https://www.akc.org/expert-advice/health/puppy-teething-and-nipping/

Donovan, L. (2019, August 30). *Leash Train Your Puppy In 5 Easy Steps.* American Kennel Club. https://www.akc.org/expert-advice/training/teach-puppy-walk-leash/

Eldredge, D. M. (2017, August 2). *How To Trim Puppy Nails Without a Fuss.* Fear Free Happy Homes. https://fearfreehappyhomes.com/how-to-trim-puppy-nails-without-a-fuss/

Farricelli, A. (2021, January 7). *How to Stop Your Dog From Biting the Leash.* PetHelpful - by Fellow Animal Lovers and Experts. https://pethelpful.com/dogs/How-to-Stop-Your-Dog-From-Biting-the-Leash

Fratt, K. (2019, April 25). *My Dog Barks Non-Stop in His Kennel – What Should I Do?* Journey Dog Training. https://journeydogtraining.com/dog-barks-nonstop-kennel/

Gibeault, S. (2019a, March 8). *The Importance of Teaching Your Puppy How to Be Alone.* American Kennel Club. https://www.akc.org/expert-advice/training/leaving-puppy-alone/

Gibeault, S. (2019b, October 25). *Why Does My Dog Dig? Identify And Channel Your Dog's Digging Instincts.* American Kennel Club. http://akc.org/expert-advice/training/why-is-my-dog-digging/

Gibeault, S. (2020a). *Training Your Dog to Ignore Distractions No Matter Where You Are.* American Kennel Club; American Kennel Club. https://www.akc.org/expert-advice/training/training-dogs-to-ignore-distractions/

Gibeault, S. (2020b, December 23). *How to Stop Your Dog From Jumping Up on People.* American Kennel Club. https://www.akc.org/expert-advice/training/how-to-stop-your-dog-from-jumping-up-on-people/

Greenwald, S. (2019, January 9). *10 Fun, Impressive Tricks You Can Teach Any Dog - Dogtime.* Dogtime. https://dogtime.com/reference/dog-training/34027-10-fun-impressive-tricks-can-teach-dog

Hansen, S. (2018, August 9). *How to Stop a Puppy from Chewing Furniture? Should You Punish Your Dog?* LabradorTrainingHQ. https://www.labradortraininghq.com/labrador-behavior/how-to-stop-a-puppy-or-dog-from-chewing/#Im_Sick

Hodgson, S. (n.d.). *How to Introduce Your Puppy to Other Family Pets.* Dummies. https://www.dummies.com/pets/dogs/how-to-introduce-your-puppy-to-other-family-pets/

Jones, E. (2019, August 16). *My Dog Is Afraid Of The Vaccum! What Can I Do To Make It Less Scary?* K9 of Mine. https://www.k9ofmine.com/dog-is-scared-of-vacuum/

Lunchick, P. (2020, February 3). *5 Simple Commands You Should Teach Your Puppy.* American Kennel Club. https://www.akc.org/expert-advice/training/teach-your-puppy-these-5-basic-commands/#sit

Mansourian, E. (2016, June 16). *American Kennel Club.* American Kennel Club. https://www.akc.org/expert-advice/health/puppy-feeding-fundamentals/

Miller, P. (2010, May 12). *How To Stop the Dog from Chasing Children.* Whole Dog Journal. https://www.whole-dog-journal.com/behavior/how-to-stop-the-dog-from-chasing-children/

PetMD. (2019, July 25). *Why Is My Dog Scared of Everything?* Www.petmd.com. https://www.petmd.com/dog/behavior/why-my-dog-scared-everything#:~:text=Lack%20of%20Socialization

Reisen, J. (2016, July 27). *House Rules for Puppies and Dogs.* American Kennel Club. https://www.akc.org/expert-advice/training/how-to-create-house-rules-for-your-new-puppy/

Reisen, J. (2020, January 28). *Bringing a Puppy Home: Help Your Puppy Adjust to a New Home.* American Kennel Club. https://www.akc.org/expert-advice/training/8-tips-to-help-your-new-puppy-adjust-to-new-home/

Shojai, A. (2011). *Introducing a New Puppy to an Older Dog.* The Spruce Pets. https://www.thesprucepets.com/introducing-dogs-and-puppies-2805078

Shojai, A. (2019, July 13). *What You Can Do to Make Your Puppy Less Scared.* The Spruce Pets. https://www.thesprucepets.com/dealing-with-a-scared-puppy-2804585

Simpawtico. (2016). *Rollover/Play Dead*. Simpawtico Training. https://www.simpawtico-training.com/download/3052/

Simpawtico Training. (n.d.). *Resource Guarding*. Simpawtico Training. https://www.simpawtico-training.com/download/4150/

Simpawtico Training. (2017). *Coprophagia (Poop Eating)*. Simpawtico Dog Training LLC. https://www.simpawtico-training.com/download/3073/

Stilwell, V. (n.d.). *Go Settle*. Victoria Stilwell Positively. Retrieved February 15, 2021, from https://positively.com/dog-behavior/basic-cues/go-settle/

Sydney. (2018, July 11). *Minding Your Pees and Poos*. Ultimate Puppy. https://ultimatepuppy.com/2018/07/11/minding-your-pees-and-poos/

The Humane Society. (2018). *Crate training 101*. The Humane Society of the United States. https://www.humanesociety.org/resources/crate-training-101

The Puppy Academy. (2020, February 24). *How to Train Your Puppy for Car Rides*. The Puppy Academy. https://www.thepuppyacademy.com/blog/2020/2/24/how-to-train-your-puppy-for-car-rides

Tyler, L. (2010, November 2). *Teaching Concepts - Duration, Distractions and Distance | IAABC Dog Blog*. Iaabc.org. https://iaabc.org/dog/teaching-concepts-duration-distractions-and-distance

Ultimate Puppy. (2015, January 30). *Games*. Ultimate Puppy. https://ultimatepuppy.com/games

Image References

Brutyo, R. (2019). Yellow Labrador retriever biting yellow tulip flower. In *Unsplash*. https://images.unsplash.com/photo-1552053831-71594a27632d?ixid=MXwxMjA3fDB8MHxwaG90by1wYWdlfHx8fGVufDB8fHw%3D&ixlib=rb-1.2.1&auto=format&fit=crop&w=312&q=80

Cheng, D. (2019). Short haired white and brown puppy. In *Unsplash*. https://images.unsplash.com/photo-1571562110290-08784605c218?ixid=MXwxMjA3fDB8MHxwaG90by1wYWdlfHx8fGVufDB8fHw%3D&ixlib=rb-1.2.1&auto=format&fit=crop&w=1950&q=80

Cook, S. (2019). Free animal image. In *Unsplash*. https://images.unsplash.com/photo-1565708097881-bbf4ecf47cc1?ixid=MXwxMjA3fDB8MHxwaG90by1wYWdlfHx8fGVufDB8fHw%3D&ixlib=rb-1.2.1&auto=format&fit=crop&w=334&q=80

Deluvio, C. (2017). Black puppy looking at cupcakes. In *Unsplash*. https://images.unsplash.com/photo-1511028897949-27b3f9f-7924d?ixid=MXwxMjA3fDB8MHxwaG90by1wYWdlfHx8fGVufDB8fHw%3D&ixlib=rb-1.2.1&auto=format&fit=crop&w=724&q=80

Dudkova, A. (2020). Black short coated puppy on white and red textile. In *Unsplash*. https://images.unsplash.com/photo-1586890723263-ebccd1879acc?ixid=MXwxMjA3fDB8MHxwaG90by1wYWdlfHx8fGVufDB8fHw%3D&ixlib=rb-1.2.1&auto=format&fit=crop&w=1789&q=80

Elvis, S. (2018). Brown dog sleeping on brown couch. In *Unsplash*. https://images.unsplash.com/photo-1529487934949-a69b5d68df88?ixid=MXwxMjA3fDB8MHxwaG90by1wYWdlfHx8fGVufDB8fHw%3D&ixlib=rb-1.2.1&auto=format&fit=crop&w=1949&q=80

Estremera, E. (2018). Black and brown daschund standing in box. In *Unsplash*. https://images.unsplash.com/photo-1520038410233-7141be7e6f97?ixlib=rb-1.2.1&ixid=MXwxMjA3fDB8MHxwaG90by1wYWdlfHx8fGVufDB8fHw%3D&auto=format&fit=crop&w=1053&q=80

Gumustekin, B. (2017). Selective focus photography of short-coated brown puppy. In *Unsplash*. https://images.unsplash.com/photo-1507146426996-ef05306b995a?ixid=MXwxMjA3fDB8MHxwaG90by1wYWdlfHx8fGVufDB8fHw%3D&ixlib=rb-1.2.1&auto=format&fit=crop&w=1050&q=80

Images, S. (2017). Depth photography of black and white dog carry ball. In *Unsplash*. https://images.unsplash.com/photo-1508948956644-0017e845d797?ixid=MXwxMjA3fDB8MHxwaG90by1wYWdlfHx8fGVufDB8fHw%3D&ixlib=rb-1.2.1&auto=format&fit=crop&w=832&q=80

Kievskaya, D. (2018). Fawn pug biting rope. In *Unsplash*. https://images.unsplash.com/photo-1522008693277-086ad6075b78?ixid=MXwxMjA3fDB8MHxwaG90by1wYWdlfHx8fGVufDB8fHw%3D&ixlib=rb-1.2.1&auto=format&fit=crop&w=334&q=80

Kopel, T. (2020). Yellow labrador retriever puppy sitting on floor. In *Unsplash*. https://images.unsplash.com/photo-1586671267731-da2cf3ceeb80?ixlib=rb-1.2.1&ixid=MXwxMjA3fDB8MHxwaG90by1wYWdlfHx8fGVufDB8fHw%3D&auto=format&fit=crop&w=335&q=80

Lesulie, C. (2018). Two brown puppies playing on ground. In *Unsplash*. https://images.unsplash.com/photo-1524487225818-c6acacb24d4e?ixid=MXwxMjA3fDB8MHxwaG90by1wYWdlfHx8fGVufDB8fHw%3D&ixlib=rb-1.2.1&auto=format&fit=crop&w=926&q=80

Lincoln, D. (2018). Short-coated tan dog. In *Unsplash*. https://images.un-splash.com/photo-1541108476383-81a896c2e478?ixid=MXwx-MjA3fDB8MHxwaG90by1wYWdlfHx8fGVufDB8fHw%3D&ix-lib=rb-1.2.1&auto=format&fit=crop&w=700&q=80

Maas, D. (2018). White puppy rolling on green grass. In *Unsplash*. https://images.unsplash.com/photo-1529906920574-628dc1e-49f5a?ixid=MXwxMjA3fDB8MHxwaG-90by1wYWdlfHx8fGVufDB8fHw%3D&ixlib=rb-1.2.1&auto=-format&fit=crop&w=1047&q=80

Middleton, M. (2020). Black pug on white textile. In *Unsplash*. https://images.unsplash.com/photo-1604813247788-621515426504?ix-id=MXwxMjA3fDB8MHxwaG-90by1wYWdlfHx8fGVufDB8fHw%3D&ixlib=rb-1.2.1&auto=-format&fit=crop&w=1932&q=80

Podilnyk, A. (2019). Shallow focus photo of devil mask Siberian husky. In *Unsplash*. https://images.unsplash.com/photo-1566903451935-7e8835ed3e97?ixid=MXwxM-jA3fDB8MHxwaG90by1wYWdlfHx8fGVufDB8fHw%3D&ix-lib=rb-1.2.1&auto=format&fit=crop&w=1050&q=80

Romero, A. (2021). White poodle puppy on purple textile. In *Unsplash*. https://images.unsplash.com/photo-1609896372384-3902df-4773fa?ixid=MXwxMjA3fDB8MHxwaG-90by1wYWdlfHx8fGVufDB8fHw%3D&ixlib=rb-1.2.1&auto=-format&fit=crop&w=967&q=80

Sandoz, G. (2019). Short coated brown puppy. In *Unsplash*. https://images.unsplash.com/photo-1550085146-e2181eb8fb82?ixid=MXwxM-jA3fDB8MHxwaG90by1wYWdlfHx8fGVufDB8fHw%3D&ix-lib=rb-1.2.1&auto=format&fit=crop&w=1050&q=80

Street, J. (2018). Dog biting brown wood on road. In *Unsplash*. https://images.unsplash.com/photo-1514984879728-be0af-f75a6e8?ixlib=rb-1.2.1&ixid=MXwxMjA3fDB8MHxwaG90by-1wYWdlfHx8fGVufDB8fHw%3D&auto=format&fit=crop&-w=1952&q=80

van den Berg, A. (2020). White and black shih tzu puppy. In *Unsplash*. https://images.unsplash.com/photo-1602582772781-82e55ac-cd83b?ixid=MXwxMjA3fDB8MHxwaG-90by1wYWdlfHx8fGVufDB8fHw%3D&ixlib=rb-1.2.1&auto=-format&fit=crop&w=1050&q=80

Printed in Great Britain
by Amazon